**Bush
Theatre**

Strange Fruit
by Caryl Phillips

12 June – 27 July 2019
Bush Theatre, London

b

Cast

Errol	**Jonathan Ajayi**
Vivian	**Rakie Ayola**
Vernice	**Debra Michaels**
Shelley	**Tilly Steele**
Alvin	**Tok Stephens**

Creative Team

Playwright	**Caryl Phillips**
Director	**Nancy Medina**
Designer	**Max Johns**
Lighting Designer	**Sally Ferguson**
Sound Designer	**Xana**
Fight and Intimacy Director	**Yarit Dor**
Costume Supervisor	**Rianna Azoro**
Voice Coach	**Joel Trill**
Wigs, Hair and Makeup	**Cynthia De La Rosa**
Production Manager	**Phil Buckley**
Company Stage Manager	**Rike Berg**
Assistant Stage Manager	**Hanne Schulpe**

Cast

JONATHAN AJAYI
Theatre credits include: *The Brother's Size* (The Young Vic).
Television credits include: *Noughts and Crosses* (BBC), *The Drifters*.

RAKIE AYOLA
Theatre credits include: *The Half God of Rainfall* (Kiln Theatre), *Leave To Remain* (Lyric Hammersmith), *Harry Potter and the Cursed Child* (The Palace Theatre), *The Rest of Your Life* (Bush Theatre), *King Lear* (Royal Exchange/Talawa), *Crave/ 4:48 Psychosis* (Sheffield Crucible), *The Curious Incident of the Dog in the Night Time* (Apollo Theatre), *The Winter's Tale* (RSC), *The Next Room* (Theatre Royal, Bath), *Welcome To Thebes* (National Theatre), *Twelfth Night* (Bristol Old Vic), *Dido Queen of Carthage* (Globe), *King Hedley II* (Tricycle Theatre) and *Hamlet* and *Twelfth Night* (Birmingham Rep).

Television credits include: *Noughts and Crosses*, *Shetland*, *Brexit: The Uncivil War*, *Flowers*, *Vera*, *Code of A Killer*, *Midsomer Murders*, *Under Milk Wood*, *Black Mirror*, *Stella*, *Silent Witness*, *My Almost Famous Family*, *Doctor Who*, *Holby City*, *Sea of Souls*, *Canterbury Tales* and *Being April*.

Film credits include: *Been So Long*, *Dredd*, *Now is Good*, *Sahara*, *The I Inside*, *Great Moments in Aviation* and *The Secret Laughter of Women*.

DEBRA MICHAELS
Theatre credits include: *The Man of La Mancha* (English National Opera), *The Curious Incident of the Dog in the Night Time* (National Theatre/UK Tour), *Red Snapper* (Belgrade Theatre, Coventry), *Cinderella* (Lyric Hammersmith), *Cinderella* (Watford Palace), *Chicago* and *Catwalk* (The Tricycle), *Carmen Jones* (Old Vic/European tour), *Porgy And Bess* (Glyndebourne/Covent Garden), *Barnum*, *Little Shop Of Horrors*, *Soul Train*, *Cinderella*, *Tricksters' Payback*, *Jekyll and Hyde*, *Four Note Opera*, *Sleeping Beauty*, *A Midsummer Night's Dream* and *The Bottle Imp*.

Television credits include: *Broken*, *Doctors*, *Holby City*, *The Lodge*, The South Bank Show Special, *The Real McCoy*, The Laurence Olivier Awards, The Evening Standard Awards and *Rites*.

Debra has worked as a Musical Director on *The Wiz* (Riverside Studios) and *Singing Bridges* (LWT), and as vocal coach on McDonalds *Our Town Story* (The Dome). She also co-created and choreographed *The Wedding Dance* which received its premiere at Bolton Octagon prior to a tour.

TILLY STEELE

Tilly grew up in Barrow-in-Furness, Cumbria. She is a graduate of the University of Sheffield and the Bristol Old Vic Theatre School. This is her first time performing at the Bush Theatre.

Theatre credits include: *Barnbow Canaries* (Leeds Playhouse), *Teechers* (Cheltenham Everyman) and *Road* (Circomedia).

Television credits include: *Doctor Who* (BBC), *Victoria* (ITV) and *Career of Evil* (BBC).

TOK STEPHEN

Theatre credits include: *Summer and Smoke* (Almeida/Duke of York's Theatre), *Revenants* (Pleasance), *Boudica* (Globe Theatre) and *Scuttlers*, *Summerfolk* and *Macbeth* (RADA).

Television credits include: *Grantchester*, *Letters* (short film).

Creative Team

CARYL PHILLIPS – PLAYWRIGHT

Caryl Phillips was born in St. Kitts and brought up in England. He has written extensively for stage, radio, television and the screen. His first play, *Strange Fruit*, premiered at the Sheffield Crucible Theatre in 1980, with subsequent productions in London and at the Liverpool Playhouse. *Where There is Darkness* and *The Shelter* both premiered at the Lyric Theatre, Hammersmith. In 2007 his adaptation of Simon Schama's *Rough Crossings* for the stage toured Britain. He collaborated with Peter Hall, writing and co-producing a three-hour film of his first novel, *The Final Passage*, for Channel Four, for whom he also wrote the film *Playing Away*. In 2001 he adapted V. S. Naipaul's *The Mystic Masseur* for Merchant Ivory Films. He is the author of numerous books of non-fiction and fiction. *Dancing in the Dark* won the 2006 PEN Open Book Award, and *A Distant Shore* was longlisted for the Booker Prize and won the 2004 Commonwealth Writers Prize. His other awards include the Martin Luther King Memorial Prize for *The European Tribe*, a Lannan Literary Award, a Guggenheim Fellowship, and the James Tait Black Memorial Prize for *Crossing the River*, which was also shortlisted for the Booker Prize. He is a contributor to newspapers and magazines on both sides of the Atlantic, a Fellow of the Royal Society of Literature, and holds honorary doctorates from a number of universities. He has taught at universities in Singapore, Ghana, Sweden and Barbados, and is currently Professor of English at Yale University. His most recent novel, *A View of the Empire at Sunset*, was published in 2018.

NANCY MEDINA – DIRECTOR

Nancy Medina is originally from Brooklyn, New York City, and currently based in Bristol. She is the 2018 RTST Sir Peter Hall Director Award winner and will be collaborating with Royal & Derngate and English Touring Theatre on August Wilson's

Two Trains Running in the autumn of 2019. In 2017 she was a Genesis Director at the Young Vic. She is an acting tutor at the Bristol Old Vic Theatre School and Course Leader for a post-16 Professional Acting Diploma at Boomsatsuma. Her directing credits include: *The Half God of Rainfall* (Kiln Theatre/Fuel/Birmingham Rep), *Flesh* (NT Connections/Bristol Old Vic), *Curried Goat and Fish Fingers* (Bristol Old Vic), *Collective Rage: A Play in 5 Betties* (Royal Welsh College of Music and Drama), *When They Go Low* (NT Connections/Sherman Theatre), *Yellowman* (Young Vic), *Romeo and Juliet* (GB Theatre), *As You Like it* (GB Theatre), *Dogtag* (Theatre West), *Strawberry & Chocolate* (Tobacco Factory Theatres), *Dutchman* (Tobacco Factory Theatres) and *Persistence of Memory* (Rondo Theatre).

MAX JOHNS – DESIGNER

Max Johns trained in theatre design at Bristol Old Vic Theatre School and was the recipient of a BBC Performing Arts Fellowship in 2015. Prior to this he worked for a number of years as a designer in Germany. His most recent UK productions include: *Rust* (Hightide/Bush Theatre), *The Half God Of Rainfall* (Kiln Theatre/Fuel/Birmingham Rep), *Wendy and Peter Pan* (Royal Lyceum Edinburgh), *Kes* and *Random* (Leeds Playhouse), *Utility* (Orange Tree Theatre), *Buggy Baby* (Yard Theatre), *Yellowman* (Young Vic), *Baddies* (Synergy Theatre Project), *Fidelio* (London Philharmonic Orchestra), *Enron* (The Egg), *There Shall Be Fireworks* (Plasticine Men), *Twelfth Night* (Orange Tree Theatre), *Life Raft*, *Medusa* and *Under a Cardboard Sea* (Bristol Old Vic), *Strawberry & Chocolate* (Tobacco Factory Theatre), *Infinity Pool* (Bedlam), *Bucket List* (Theatre Ad Infinitum), *Hamlet* and *All's Well That Ends Well* (Tobacco Factory Theatre). Max has also had work produced at the V&A and Theatre Royal Bath. Forthcoming productions include *King John* at the Royal Shakespeare Company, directed by Eleanor Rhode.

SALLY FERGUSON – LIGHTING DESIGNER

Sally's credits include: *Snow White* (Ovalhouse), *An Adventure* (Bush Theatre), *Jess And Joe Forever* (Orange Tree), *The Two Boroughs Project* (Young Vic), *Sweet Charity* (Manchester Royal Exchange), *We Wait In Joyful Hope, And Then Come The Nightjars, Many Moons* (Theatre 503), *Shiver, Lost In Yonkers* (Watford Palace Theatre), *The Sleeping Beauties* (Sherman Cymru), *As You Like It, Floyd Collins* (Southwark Playhouse), *Hag, The Girl With The Iron Claws* (Wrong Crowd/ Soho Theatre), *Microcosm* (Soho Theatre), *The Imagination Museum* (UK tour), *Slowly* (Riverside Studios), *Cosi fan Tutte* (Village Underground), *The Devils Festival* (The Print Room), *The Marriage Of Figaro* (Wilton's Music Hall), *The Wonder! A Woman Keeps A Secret* (BAC).

XANA – SOUND DESIGNER

Xana is a Offie-nominated sound designer, a live loop musician, modular synthesist, installation maker and writer. Theatre credits include: *Ivan and the Dogs* (Young Vic), *Grey* (Ovalhouse), *Pink Lemonade* (Gate Theatre), *Burgerz* (touring), *Just Another Day and Night* (Ovalhouse), *Mapping* (Brent Festival), *Blood Knot* (Orange Tree Theatre); *SEX SEX MEN MEN* (Pecs Drag Kings/The Yard); *Noughts and Crosses* (Pilot Theatre/Derby Theatre), *Burgerz* (Hackney Showroom), *Obama and Me* (Talawa/Camden Peoples Theatre), *Black Holes* (The Place), *Hive City Legacy* (Roundhouse), *Half-breed* (Soho Theatre), *Primetime* (Royal Court). Xana's work focuses on archives and embodying our future narratives and memories using tech to creating interactive spaces and manifest new visions of blackness. Xana is an Associate Artist at Ovalhouse and is featured on the award-winning composition Afronaut, from the album Driftglass by SEED Ensemble.

Thank You's

Michael McMillan
Mathew Clowes (Hull Truck)
Kay Buckley (Bolton Octagon)
Mike Redley (York Theatre Royal)
Mark Distin Webster (Royal Exchange Theatre)
Kieran Myles (RT Scenic)
Ralph Tricker

Carpet provided and fitted by E. Mills & Son Linoleum Ltd based in Shepherd's Bush Market

Bush Theatre

Bush Theatre

We make theatre
for London. Now.

The Bush is a world-famous home for new plays
and an internationally renowned champion of
playwrights. We discover, nurture and produce
the best new writers from the widest range of
backgrounds from our home in a distinctive corner
of west London.

The Bush has won over 100 awards and developed
an enviable reputation for touring its acclaimed
productions nationally and internationally.

We are excited by exceptional new voices,
stories and perspectives – particularly those with
contemporary bite which reflect the vibrancy of
British culture now.

Located in the newly renovated old library on
Uxbridge Road in the heart of Shepherd's Bush,
the theatre houses two performance spaces, a
rehearsal room and the lively Library Bar.

 Supported by ARTS COUNCIL ENGLAND h&f hammersmith & fulham

bushtheatre.co.uk

THANK YOU

The Bush Theatre would like to thank all its supporters whose valuable contributions have helped us to create a platform for our future and to promote the highest quality new writing, develop the next generation of creative talent, lead innovative community engagement work and champion diversity.

LONE STAR
Gianni Alen-Buckley
Michael Alen-Buckley
Rafael & Anne-Helene Biosse Duplan
Alice Findlay
Charles Holloway
Miles Morland

HANDFUL OF STARS
Dawn & Gary Baker
Charlie Bigham
Judy Bollinger
Clive & Helena Butler
Grace Chan
Clare & Chris Clark
Clyde Cooper
Sue Fletcher
Richard & Jane Gordon
Priscilla John
Simon & Katherine Johnson
Philippa Seal & Philip Jones QC
Joanna Kennedy
V&F Lukey
Robert Ledger & Sally Mousdale
Georgia Oetker
Philip & Biddy Percival
Clare Rich
Joana & Henrik Schliemann
Lesley Hill & Russ Shaw
van Tulleken Family
and one anonymous donor.

RISING STARS
Nicholas Alt
Mark Bentley
David Brooks
Catharine Browne
Matthew Byam Shaw
Tim & Andrea Clark
Sarah Clarke
Claude & Susie Cochin de Billy
Lois Cox
Susie Cuff
Matthew Cushen
Philippa Dolphin
John Fraser
Jack Gordon & Kate Lacy
Hugh & Sarah Grootenhuis
Jessica Ground
Thea Guest
Patrick Harrison
Roberta Jaffe-Wilcockson
Ann & Ravi Joseph
Davina & Malcolm Judelson
Miggy Littlejohns
Isabella Macpherson

RISING STARS (continued)
Liz & Luke Mayhew
Michael McCoy
Judith Mellor
Caro Millington
Dan & Laurie Mucha
Mark & Anne Paterson
Barbara Prideaux
Emily Reeve
Renske & Marion
Saleem & Alexandra Siddiqi
Brian Smith
Peter Tausig
Guy Vincent & Sarah Mitchell
Trish Wadley
Amanda Waggott
and three anonymous donors.

SPONSORS & SUPPORTERS
AKA
Alen-Buckley LLP
Gianni & Michael Alen-Buckley
Jeremy Attard Manche
Bill & Judy Bollinger
Edward Bonham Carter
Martin Bowley
Duke & Duchess of Buccleuch
The Hon Mrs Louise Burness
Sir Charles & Lady Isabella Burrell
Philip & Tita Byrne
CHK Charities Limited
Peppe & Quentin Ciardi
Joanna & Hadyn Cunningham
Leo & Grega Daly
Patrick & Mairead Flaherty
Sue Fletcher
The Hon Sir Rocco Forte
The Hon Portia Forte
Mark Franklin
The Gatsby Charitable Foundation
The Right Hon Piers Gibson
Farid & Emile Gragour
Victoria Gray
John Gordon
Vivienne Guinness
Melanie Hall
The Headley Trust
Brian Heyworth
Lesley Hill & Russ Shaw
Michael Holland & Denise O'Donoghue
Charles Holloway
Graham & Amanda Hutton
James Gorst Architects Ltd.
Simon & Katherine Johnson
Tarek & Diala Khlat

SPONSORS & SUPPORTERS (continued)
Bernard Lambilliotte
Marion Lloyd
The Lord Forte Foundation
Peter & Bettina Mallinson
Mahoro Charitable Trust
James Christopher Miller
Mitsui Fodosan (U.K.) Ltd
Alfred Munkenbeck III
Nick Hern Books
Georgia Oetker
RAB Capital
Kevin Pakenham
Sir Howard Panter
Joanna Prior
Josie Rourke
Lady Susie Sainsbury
Barry Serjent
Tim & Catherine Score
Search Foundation
Richard Sharp
Susie Simkins
Edward Snape & Marilyn Eardley
Michael & Sarah Spencer
Stanhope PLC
Ross Turner
The Syder Foundation
van Tulleken Family
Johnny & Dione Verulam
Robert & Felicity Waley-Cohen
Elizabeth Wigoder
Philip Wooller
Danny Wyler
and three anonymous donors.

TRUSTS AND FOUNDATIONS
The Andrew Lloyd Webber Foundation
The Boris Karloff Foundation
The Boshier-Hinton Foundation
The Bruce Wake Charitable Trust
The Chapman Charitable Trust
The City Bridge Trust
Cockayne—Grants for the Arts
The John S Cohen Foundation
The Daisy Trust
The Equity Charitable Trust
Esmée Fairbairn Foundation
Fidelio Charitable Trust
Foyle Foundation
Garfield Weston Foundation
Garrick Charitable Trust
Hammersmith United Charities
Heritage of London Trust
John Lyon's Charity
The J Paul Getty Jnr Charitable Trust

TRUSTS AND FOUNDATIONS (continued)
The John Thaw Foundation
The Kirsten Scott Memorial Trust
The Leverhulme Trust
The London Community Foundation
Margaret Guido's Charitable Trust
The Martin Bowley Charitable Trust
The Monument Trust
The Noel Coward Foundation
Paul Hamlyn Foundation
Peter Wolff Foundation
Pilgrim Trust
The Royal Victoria Hall Foundation
Sir John Cass's Foundation
Stavros Niarchos Foundation
The Theatres Trust
Viridor Credits
The Williams Charitable Trust
Western Riverside
Worshipful Company of Mercers
Environmental Fund
The Wolfson Foundation
and one anonymous donor.

CORPORATE SPONSORS AND MEMBERS
The Agency (London) Ltd
Dorsett Shepherds Bush
Drama Centre London
Fever Tree
The Groucho Club
THE HOXTON
Philip Wooller
Westfield London

PUBLIC FUNDING

If you are interested in finding out how to be involved, please visit **bushtheatre.co.uk/support-us** or email **development@bushtheatre.co.uk** or call **020 8743 3584**.

Bush Theatre

PASSING THE BATON

Rediscovering the artists of colour who carved their way through British playwriting with distinction

Passing the Baton is a three-year initiative by the Bush Theatre to reacquaint theatre-goers with playwrights who have been forgotten, are out of print and whose plays are not revived despite their status as critically acclaimed artists.

At the same time, a promising emerging writer of colour will be given a full length commission for the main house alongside mentoring to develop their work. In this way we will be passing the baton between established writers and emerging writers of colour.

In 2018 we introduced new audiences to Leave Taking by Winsome Pinnock and the first Passing the Baton commission went to Kalungi Ssebandeke.

In 2019, we are proud to present a revival of Strange Fruit by Caryl Phillips, a playwright and educator who has paved the way for writers and artists not just here in London, but in the US as well.

The Bush is grateful to the numerous industry figures who provided their recommendations on the extraordinary body of work from 20th century British writers of colour.

STRANGE FRUIT

Caryl Phillips

STRANGE FRUIT

OBERON BOOKS
LONDON

WWW.OBERONBOOKS.COM

First published in 1981 by Amber Lane Press

This edition published in 2019 by Oberon Books Ltd
521 Caledonian Road, London N7 9RH
Tel: +44 (0) 20 7607 3637 / Fax: +44 (0) 20 7607 3629
e-mail: info@oberonbooks.com
www.oberonbooks.com

PB ISBN: 9781786827845
E ISBN: 9781786827876

Cover design by Studio Doug
Cover photography by Bronwen Sharp

Printed and bound by 4EDGE Limited, Hockley, Essex, UK.
eBook conversion by Lapiz Digital Services, India.

Visit www.oberonbooks.com to read more about all our books and to buy them. You will
also find features, author interviews and news of any author events, and you can sign up for
e-newsletters so that you're always first to hear about our new releases.

Printed on FSC® accredited paper

10 9 8 7 6 5 4 3 2 1

For Catherine

Preface

I wrote *Strange Fruit* during the autumn of 1979. I had graduated from university in June of the same year with a desire to write, but this was long before the recent proliferation of Creative Writing classes and graduate courses. Therefore, the path to becoming a writer was very unclear; but as far as I could make out, it seemed to involve avoiding the pitfall of taking an actual job and instead hustling together some kind of piecemeal income doing bits of freelance reviewing, or writing short articles, plus, in my case, signing on the dole. I therefore passed the autumn of 1979 in a cramped flat in Edinburgh where, when not struggling to earn some money, I started to teach myself to type.

The three years that I had spent at university (1976-1979) were prefaced by the 1976 Notting Hill Carnival riots and the rise of an impatient militancy among my generation, a restlessness that was given impetus by the triumphant tour of the West Indies cricket team during that long, hot, summer. As a result, I went to off to study as a resolute and focused eighteen-year-old. Three years later, my generation had become even more vocal and uncompromising in their determination not to become marginalized and ignored by British society in the manner which they felt had been visited upon their parents' generation. The twenty-one-year-old young man who stepped away from university in 1979 had the soundtrack of Linton Kwesi Johnson's *Dread Beat an' Blood* in his head, and a definite understanding that the election of Mrs Thatcher in June 1979 meant that battle lines were about to be drawn for many people in British society, including coal miners, the gay community and, of course, the Black and Asian population. I retreated to Edinburgh and began to write.

I secretly harboured the ambition of one day writing a novel, but this seemed such a far-off and somewhat fanciful idea. In the meantime, because I felt that I *did* have things to say, and because I had directed plays as a student and understood a little about the grammar of dramatic writing, I turned to the theatre. I did so in the hope that the subject matter that felt so urgent to me might somehow be expressed on the stage.

Forty years later, I have now re-read the play; I have also refocused my gaze on twenty-first century Britain and come to the not entirely surprising conclusion that some things never change. First, parents and children are always going to live with the danger of becoming the victims of hurtful misunderstandings born of shame and fear. We, the children, and we, the parents, will habitually offer each other silence in place of dialogue and honesty. It is often difficult to talk, but such reticence can lead to distrust and confusion which, if not properly arrested, can quickly atrophy into despair. Second, Britain's 'betrayal' of those citizens of the empire who arrived with a desire to contribute in the post-war years continues to this day. But more than this – it is not just black and brown people who feel demeaned and humiliated by the country; Britain's recent decision to leave the European Economic Community has left many, of all ethnic, racial and religious backgrounds, feeling bemused, angry and suddenly invisible in a country they considered to be home.

A writer writes because they have something to say. In my own case, I persevere because my subject matter – that unpredictable reciprocity of human strength and weakness (what William Faulkner called 'the human heart in conflict with itself') – continues to preoccupy me; and I also press on because I continue to believe that I still have something to say about the socio-political world which can often intrude with devastating speed and forcefully shatter the emotional fragility that is at the centre of our being. It is not for me to say what the play is about, but on re-reading it I am humbled to discover five courageous people who are striving very hard, in their own ways, to survive. I respect each and every one of them.

Caryl Phillips
May 2019

Characters

(In order of appearance)

MOTHER
VERNICE
SHELLEY
ERROL
ALVIN

Act One
Scene One: Monday. Late afternoon
Scene Two: Monday. Later that night

Act Two
Scene One: Tuesday. Early morning
Scene Two: Tuesday. Afternoon

Act Three
Scene One: Tuesday. Evening

A note on the language
The language in *Strange Fruit* has to be a careful mixture of West Indian English (patois), Standard English, and English working-class regional dialect. In the language one should be able to detect the socio-cultural confusion which undermines any immediate hopes of harmony within the body politic of the family.

Act One

SCENE ONE

The action takes place in the front room of the Marshalls' terraced house in one of England's inner city areas. Whilst the district is not a ghetto, it is hardly suburbia. The room is cramped but comfortable and tidy. In the D.R. wall is a door which leads to the hall, and subsequently to the front door. In the back wall (slightly right of centre) is another door, which can be concealed by the drawing of a curtain. This door leads upstairs to the bedrooms and the bathroom. In the D.L. wall is a door which leads to the kitchen. It is one of those that slides open, rather than pulls or pushes open. The main items of furniture are as follows: against the back wall there is a heavy sideboard, on top of which sits a brightly crocheted coverlet, a large plastic punchbowl and ladle, a yellow glass vase containing plastic flowers, and a box of paper tissues. D.R. is a cabinet full of crockery that has never been, and never will be used. In the centre of the display is a plate commemorating the Queen's Silver Jubilee. The cabinet also contains a few bottles of spirits, and on top of it sit the family photographs. D.L. is a small table underneath which there are some albums. A small stereo sits on top with the speakers placed on the floor either side, thus completing this nest of music. In the centre of the room is an imitation black leather settee with orange yellow cushions. U.L. slightly is the armchair to match. The room is completed by the television, which is D.L. by the stereo. As to the surroundings: the wallpaper is tasteless, and on the wall hang the usual trinkets. Sub-Athena prints, a circular mirror with a gnarled plastic, imitation brass border, and those birds made of pottery which are so arranged as to make it appear that they are migrating for the winter as they fly away, one after the other. The windows on the world are in the fourth wall. Acknowledgement of their presence is not necessary. As I said, the room is cramped, even claustrophobic, but tidy.

Lights up. 5 p.m. We hear a key in the front door and then the door slam. Enter MOTHER carrying a shopping bag. She shuts the door behind her, leans against it and sighs deeply. She looks like she has never had

11

a day's rest in her life but is still neat and immaculately turned out. She is in her late forties and both thinks and acts thoroughly, albeit with a somewhat premature autumnal serenity. Still through a small chink in her armour one can sense despair. She knows that most of what is going to happen is inevitable so she prepares for the worst, as ever. Clearly the twin concepts of love and fear are at the heart of her character. She puts down the bag, takes off her coat and drapes it over the back of the armchair. She moves across to the settee and sits alone with her thoughts for a moment.

VERNICE: *(From the kitchen.)* Girl, you back home yet? Vivien you hear me?

(She shuts the back door and comes through the open sliding door into the front room. VERNICE is portly, about the same age as MOTHER, and wears a brightly coloured headscarf, Scholl sandals, no tights, which, together with her happy-go-lucky demeanour, suggests an easy attitude to life, one which she likes to project. She enjoys unsettling people, but not in a vindictive manner. Humorously 'loud' at times, she enjoys her telly. For her, England's not so much the enemy. Life has always been a struggle for survival. England is just the place where things have crumbled, where she has seen her life move from a very healthy top gear to a very insecure first. She sees MOTHER and sucks her teeth.)

Girl, why yuh no answer me, nuh?

MOTHER: I was about to. You didn't give me time.

VERNICE: Girl, me give you plenty time. You ain't hear me calling you or something, nuh.

MOTHER: I was about to, but I've only just got home from school.

VERNICE: You too wicked, you know.

MOTHER: I thought I locked that back door before I left this morning.

12

VERNICE: Errol open it for me before he go out.

MOTHER: To go where?

VERNICE: Me ain't ask. He come a big man now, or you ain't notice. *(Sucks her teeth. Pause.)* Alvin coming back tonight? Me see all him things them on the line.

MOTHER: Where are they?

VERNICE: Girl, what you think it is me do with them, nuh? Me put them in the flickin' kitchen basket.

MOTHER: Tomorrow.

VERNICE: What you talking about tomorrow for, eh? Me put them in the damn basket today, girl.

MOTHER: Alvin is coming back tomorrow. I'm going to iron his clothes today.

VERNICE: Well, why you not say so instead of friggin' me up so.

MOTHER: *(Sighs.)* Would you like some tea, Vernice?

VERNICE: Uh hur. Come, lemme give you a hand, nuh. *(Makes no attempt to do so.)*

MOTHER: No, it's alright. *(She gets up and goes to the kitchen.)*

The electric kettle is still broken so I'm going to have to boil the water in a pan. It won't take long if that's alright with madam.

VERNICE: It's alright.

MOTHER: Is everything here?

VERNICE: *(Sucks her teeth.)* Girl, what you meaning now? Your arse beginning to sound off like twenty questions or something.

MOTHER: In the laundry basket?

VERNICE: What happen? You think me want to thief off some uh you son's clothes for me daughter to come dress up in them? *(Sucks her teeth.)*

MOTHER: Good God, Vernice, I just wondered if Errol had taken any away for I haven't had time to do his washing yet. I'm not accusing you of anything.

VERNICE: Well, me ain't know, girl. All me did was to bring in the basket and then me leave the boy to do his own thing, or whatever it is them all like to do.

MOTHER: I see.

VERNICE: Anyway, Alvin ain't the type of boy to mash up his own brother for thieving a pair uh socks. The pair of them getting on just fine in all the time me know them. Good spars.

MOTHER: Good what?

VERNICE: Good spars. Girl, you ain't up with the times, as usual.

(MOTHER comes through with two cups of tea – no saucers.)

MOTHER: Well, Alvin can get nasty at times about his things. He gets a bit overbearing.

VERNICE: Girl, you too bad sometimes. Why you don't leave the boys them alone, nuh? They still young and got plenty time for all that kinda thing. You should just be grateful that the pair uh them managing to keep themselves outa trouble with the police and thing.

MOTHER: Should be glad of what? Grateful for what! Vernice, my children have never been in any kind of trouble. My children are qualified, they have O-Levels and A-Levels and have both been to college, and you're telling me that I should be happy that they are managing to keep out of trouble.

VERNICE: *(Sucks her teeth.)* Girl, you know it mus' be hard for they with you all come a teacher and you always coming down so hard on they when they so young still. You too friggin' rough on they, you know.

MOTHER: I think I'm the best judge of that. Look Vernice, I've got work to do and I'm tired.

VERNICE: Me arse, I come round here to ask one favour of you but if you want me go…

MOTHER: Then for heaven's sake ask.

VERNICE: It's Charmain.

MOTHER: Well?

VERNICE: She ain't talking to me.

MOTHER: Again! Well, she must be saying something.

VERNICE: When Charmain decide she ain't talking, she ain't saying nothing to nobody, you hear me.

MOTHER: *(Sighs.)* How long's this been going on?

VERNICE: Only two or three days but Lord, with only me and she alone in the house it feel like weeks. Me think she must be missing having a father.

MOTHER: But, Vernice, it's eight years since Wilfred passed on.

VERNICE: You think I don't know that?

MOTHER: I'm sorry. What would you like me to do?

VERNICE: Girl, me ain't know, but I thought with you being a teacher and use to kids playing up and thing that mebbe you could talk to she and get some sense in she damn head.

MOTHER: Well, how's she doing at school?

VERNICE: Me ain't know girl. Last parents' evening she have is about two years ago now. She doing alright then.

MOTHER: Rubbish!

VERNICE: What you mean 'rubbish'? I tell you she doing alright then, or mebbe you think it just you all who is able to come intelligent, eh? Well don't come none of you hoity-toity ways with me girl, for me know you all long time and don't let you arse forget it, nuh.

MOTHER: Vernice, parents' evening is twice a year, and now she's in the fifth form you should be getting a fortnightly report.

VERNICE: And where you say me supposed to be getting all this from?

MOTHER: Well, hasn't she been giving you one?

VERNICE: *(Sucks her teeth.)* Giving me one what, girl? All she give me is one set uh filthy looks after the other. *(Pause.)* You think me oughta go and ask she for it?

MOTHER: Naturally. Look Vernice, you might have a better chance of finding out why she's acting like she's doing if you have a look at it.

VERNICE: I tell you me ain't even know she got the blasted thing. Look the hell, me going to have to ask she for it. *(Gets up.)* Lord, she ain't going to like this, for sure.

MOTHER: She's not supposed to like it. It's her duty for God's sake.

VERNICE: Me going ask she.

(VERNICE goes out via the kitchen. MOTHER rises and takes the two cups into the kitchen. She picks up her bag of shopping en route. She comes back through, after a few moments, with the basket full of

ALVIN's, clothes and begins to sort through them. We hear the back door slam. Re-enter VERNICE with the report.)

MOTHER: Did you get it?

VERNICE: Me have it. The girl just throw it at me and storm out the house.

MOTHER: Well open it then. Go ahead.

VERNICE: You open it.

(MOTHER reluctantly takes it, opens it, and begins to read.)

Well?

MOTHER: She's not doing too well.

VERNICE: What?

MOTHER: Well, you do know that they've moved her out of the GCE into the CSE stream, which means that her chances of ending up with an HND or even a BSc rather than just an OND are greatly diminished.

VERNICE: Fockin' CSE, GCE, CND, this that and the other is just one seta flickin' initial to me. What the hell the matter with she?

MOTHER: Well, nothing that a...

VERNICE: Nothing? If me can't talk to me own daughter then something is the matter.

MOTHER: I think you'd better go and see her teacher. She says here that she's also worried about her absenteeism.

VERNICE: What fockin' absenteeism? The girl ain't had a day off school since she eight.

MOTHER: But...

VERNICE: No fockin' but about it. I just about had she up to me back teeth. *(She stands.)*

MOTHER: Sit down, Vernice, and listen. I'll come round with you and we'll talk to her together if you like.

VERNICE: No point. She just gone off. Who the hell she think she is anyway playing absent from she school.

MOTHER: Okay, then, I'll call round tomorrow after work.

VERNICE: What you mean work tomorrow?

MOTHER: I mean what I said. Work tomorrow.

VERNICE: You mean you ain't coming out on strike with us then?

MOTHER: Vernice, what do you mean coming out on strike with 'us'. Since when have you done a day's work in your life.

VERNICE: Girl, me a widow with a house and daughter to look after. Don't forget me ain't have no man in me house either.

MOTHER: Hmmm.

VERNICE: What you say?

MOTHER: Nothing.

VERNICE: Come again.

MOTHER: I said nothing.

VERNICE: Lemme tell you girl. One day you going have to join the coloured race and you best watch you all step that nobody kick you in you arse when you decide it time you want to do so.

(Gets up.)

I going to see me affairs.

(She goes out via the kitchen. MOTHER sighs and begins to unwind again. After a few moments she hears the front doorbell.)

MOTHER: Damn!

(She wanted to be alone. She goes out to the hall and we hear her opening the front door.)

Hello Shelley. What brings you around at this time?

SHELLEY: Nothing really, Miss, except I've come to drop off these albums for Errol.

MOTHER: Well, come on in then. You don't have to wait on ceremony in this house, you know.

SHELLEY: Yeah, I know. Thanks.

(Enter MOTHER, followed by SHELLEY. She is sixteen, quietly pretty with dark brown shoulder-length hair, and she wears little make-up. She dresses with care, preferring a skirt or a dress to trousers. No jewellery or nail varnish: she doesn't need it.)

MOTHER: Well, how long has it been raining?

SHELLEY: Not long really. It only just started up again about ten minutes ago, but it's really coming down now.

MOTHER: Oh dear.

SHELLEY: But it looks like it's gonna stop, though. One of those quick blasts that you sometimes get.

MOTHER: Take off your coat and hang it up. I'll open out your umbrella in the kitchen if you like.

SHELLEY: Yeah, thanks.

(MOTHER takes the umbrella and goes off. SHELLEY raises her voice so that she can be heard.)

Anyhow Miss, it's bad enough being trapped in this place, the city I mean, without having it raining all the time.

MOTHER: *(Coming back through.)* What do you mean trapped? You're not trapped.

SHELLEY: I am Miss. Where am I gonna get the money from to catch a bus or even a train to the country or the seaside? Me mum and dad ain't half tight. They must think I can live on Biafran rations or something.

MOTHER: I see. Well, you could get a job I suppose.

SHELLEY: Yeah, but how am I gonna get some work done to pass my exams. I go out most nights as it is. If it isn't one thing it's another. *(Pause.)* And besides, I don't think Errol would like it. He's always on about a woman's place and the man being the 'hunter'.

MOTHER: The what?

SHELLEY: The 'hunter'.

MOTHER: You don't want to take any notice of that rubbish.

SHELLEY: No, I suppose not. *(Pause.)* He isn't at home is he, Miss?

MOTHER: What's the panic?

SHELLEY: Nothing.

(SHELLEY sighs. Pause.)

MOTHER: Are you feeling alright, Shelley?

SHELLEY: Course Miss, why?

(Pause. MOTHER looks closely at her.)

MOTHER: Look Shelley, is it Errol?

SHELLEY: Miss, it's just that sometimes it can get bad and he just cuts me off. God, I even have to lie sometimes about what I'm thinking in case he falls out with me.

MOTHER: What do you mean?

SHELLEY: Well, I'm going to have to, Miss. I can't help it unless I leave home for two days or something.

MOTHER: You're going to have to what?

SHELLEY: To buy and eat something British, break the strike. I'm going to have to get on a bus and what have you, 'cause I just have to. I've got to get to school and whatnot. but if I tell him that I'd done any of this then he'd kill me.

MOTHER: Don't be stupid, Shelley.

SHELLEY: Don't call me stupid, Miss. Everyone calls me stupid. Just because I'm not coloured doesn't mean I'm stupid or that I can't do anything.

MOTHER: Shelley.

SHELLEY: You don't know what it's like, Miss. To be gradually cut out of somebody's life after two years because they've suddenly decided that you're not right or something. He hardly talks to me, he hardly says anything without being right, and I hardly say anything without being wrong, and all the time it's us and them, or you and I, or our side and your side, and I can't stand it, Miss. I can't.

MOTHER: Calm down, Shelley. You came for a chat with me and I'm grateful. I'm listening.

SHELLEY: Yes Miss.

MOTHER: Listen, why don't you call it a day, then? You know, the pair of you split up. Tell him it's over.

SHELLEY: I can't.

MOTHER: Oh come off it Shelley, what do you mean you can't.

(SHELLEY begins to cry.)

Shelley, what's the matter?

SHELLEY: I'm sorry, Miss.

MOTHER: There's nothing to be sorry about, after all…

SHELLEY: Miss, I think I'm having a baby.

MOTHER: You only think you're having a baby?

SHELLEY: I'm pretty sure, Miss. I'm getting the results of my tests back tomorrow afternoon. *(Pause.)*

MOTHER: Have you told Errol?

SHELLEY: No Miss.

MOTHER: Why not?

SHELLEY: I told you, Miss. He doesn't seem to pay much attention to me these days

MOTHER: Well, he's obviously paid some attention to you.

SHELLEY: Miss…

(She begins to cry anew.)

MOTHER: I'm sorry, Shelley. What are we going to do?

SHELLEY: I don't know, Miss.

MOTHER: Well someone's going to have to tell him.

SHELLEY: Yes, Miss.

MOTHER: And you'd rather it wasn't you?

SHELLEY: It's not that, Miss. I just want to make sure first.

MOTHER: And your parents. Do they know?

SHELLEY: You're the only person I've told, Miss.

MOTHER: What about your friends?

SHELLEY: You're the only person I've told, Miss. *(Pause.)* Miss, it wasn't his fault.

MOTHER: What do you mean?

SHELLEY: I'm not on the pill, Miss.

MOTHER: Well, didn't you use some kind of protection?

SHELLEY: Miss – *(She begins to cry again.)*

MOTHER: Shelley.

SHELLEY: I told him I was on the pill, Miss.

MOTHER: You told him…Why?

SHELLEY: I had to, Miss, or he might not have wanted to keep going out with me. I can't go on the pill, Miss, because I'm Catholic and if me parents found out that I was on it they'd kill me.

MOTHER: I suppose that also rules out an abortion.

SHELLEY: I don't want to kill it, Miss. It's something to share. I can't kill it. Please Miss, I can't.

MOTHER: Alright, Shelley, I understand. It's going to be alright. I think we had both better have a drink. Brandy?

(SHELLEY nods. MOTHER gets up and crosses to the cabinet.)

It doesn't look as if there's much we can do until tomorrow then?

SHELLEY: No, Miss.

MOTHER: Are you going out tonight?

SHELLEY: I think so, Miss. Errol said he'd meet me at about eight o'clock by the club.

(MOTHER crosses and hands her the drink.)

MOTHER: Plenty of time, then. Shall I show you my album whilst we have a drink?

SHELLEY: Miss?

(MOTHER crosses and takes the album out of a bottom drawer in the sideboard.)

MOTHER: Photograph album. From home. *(Looks at watch.)* It's not even six yet so you won't be late.

SHELLEY: *(Wiping her eyes on the back of her hand.)* I know, Miss. *(Pause.)* Are there any pictures of Errol as a little boy?

MOTHER: *(Laughs.)* Plenty. *(She comes and sits down.)* Hasn't he shown you this before?

SHELLEY: No, Miss. I once sneaked out a load of pictures of me as a kid, but he just said that pictures negate progress and that was that.

MOTHER: Did you want anything in your brandy?

SHELLEY: I don't know, Miss. It's alright like this I think...

MOTHER: Fine.

(They settle down to look at the album. Almost immediately they hear the sound of a key in the door.)

SHELLEY: God, Miss, it's Errol. Tell him I only came round to drop off the records.

(She stands.)

I'd better be off now.

(MOTHER closes the album. Enter ERROL from the hall. He is carrying a large parcel in brown paper which he leans off against the back wall. ERROL is twenty-one and of medium height and build. He likes to think of himself as good-looking, but prefers not to dress in a sharp way for fear of being accused of vanity. So he dresses untidily, knowing that it's the mind that matters, but he will occasionally pin on a badge of protest only to remove it a few days later thinking that he's 'sold out'. He can't decide whether or not to grow an Afro, but nevertheless keeps his shapeless hair tidy-ish.)

ERROL: What are you doing here?

SHELLEY: It's okay. I'm just off.

ERROL: Oh great. Brilliant answer.

SHELLEY: I only came round to drop off some records. So?

MOTHER: What's the parcel?

ERROL: Oh that. It's a parcel.

(He moves and sits. Pause.)

MOTHER: Wipe your nose, Errol. How old are you now?

(Wiping his nose on his sleeves.)

ERROL: Forty-three, nearly forty-four.

(MOTHER tosses her head and gets up to put away the photograph album.)

SHELLEY: It's still alright about tonight then?

ERROL: What's that?

SHELLEY: Tonight?

ERROL: *(Gesturing with his hand.)* No, that.

MOTHER: Don't be stupid.

ERROL: Well I know what it is, but what's it doing out?

MOTHER: Shelley and I were just going to look at some pictures. *(She comes back and sits.)* I don't know why you don't take more interest.

ERROL: In what?

MOTHER: Things.

ERROL: *(Sucks his teeth.)* Pictures negate progress.

SHELLEY: I think pictures are nice.

ERROL: You would, wouldn't you?

MOTHER: Come on now, stop bickering.

ERROL: Who's bickering? We're not bickering, it's you.

MOTHER: Fine. Anyhow Shelley, if you ever want to have a look at them, you know where they are.

SHELLEY: Thanks.

ERROL: She's got her own 'roots'. What are you forcing her for?

SHELLEY: She's not forcing me.

MOTHER: No, I'm not. It's just natural to want to know something about your boyfriend's past.

ERROL: Well, I live in a world of reality.

MOTHER: Pardon?

ERROL: A world of reality and brutality.

SHELLEY: I'd best go now.

MOTHER: Look, for heaven's sake sit down, Shelley, and I'll get the pair of you some tea before you go out.

SHELLEY: I don't know if I should.

MOTHER: Oh come on, sit down. Nobody's going to bite you. I'll just see what we've got.

(She goes into the kitchen. SHELLEY sits down. Pause.)

ERROL: Me Momma goin' to cook up some goat for yer, you know that?

SHELLEY: Pardon?

MOTHER: *(Shouting through.)* Errol, stop that.

ERROL: She goin' cook up some good soulfood an' plenty yam.

MOTHER: *(Amused.)* Look Shelley, take no notice of him.

ERROL: Shelley, girl. I hopes yer knows we all eat cat food, you know. Kit-e-Kat, man, an' a big tinna Whiskas on a Sunday.

MOTHER: Errol, don't be stupid. Anyway, have you seen the price of cat food lately?

SHELLEY: What you on about? Come on, tell us.

MOTHER: *(Comes through from the kitchen.)* We're having salad, Shelley. Don't take any notice of him, he's just being silly.

ERROL: Salad! It's bloody freezing outside. It's only just stopped raining.

MOTHER: Well, I haven't got anything else to give you.

ERROL: I thought you said you were going to do some shopping today for Alvin coming back.

MOTHER: So?

ERROL: So, where is it?

27

MOTHER: It's in the kitchen. But I've only got one pair of hands you know.

ERROL: But it's turned six o'clock. It's not your hands you've been sat on for God knows how long.

MOTHER: Errol, no sooner had I set foot in the house than Vernice appeared…

ERROL: Oh God.

MOTHER: …and after I'd got rid of her, Shelley came round, not that I minded Shelley coming round, but where am I supposed to get time to cook in? I'm not a magician.

(She goes back into the kitchen.)

SHELLEY: She's right, Errol. Vernice can't half talk, you know. Remember that time I first met her an…

ERROL: Since when have you been an expert on Vernice and post-teaching fatigue?

SHELLEY: Well, she's right, isn't she?

ERROL: You haven't answered the question. Well… *(He waits impatiently then sucks his teeth.)* Hey! She came round here before.

MOTHER: I'm not deaf, Errol.

ERROL: Well, you're in there. I thought you might not hear.

MOTHER: *(Coming through.)* Well I'm in here now and I can hear perfectly well, thank you. Before when?

ERROL: Well, she came round and brought the clothes in off the line. Her and her lover man, Stanley the flying milkman.

MOTHER: What! You mean he helped her?

ERROL: Yeah. A real two-pronged attack it was. Is something the matter with that? He ain't got bugs you know. Alvin's clothes are still fit for human consumption or whatever.

MOTHER: I'm aware of the fact that Stanley hasn't got bugs. He was probably just passing, that's all.

ERROL: Oh come off it. At one o'clock in the afternoon? What milkman do you know that comes round at one in the afternoon? To deliver milk, anyway. I can just hear it now. 'Yes dear, that's right. We've got the only black milkman in Britain, but the unfortunate thing is he can't get out of bed before noon, and he doesn't start his round till after one, poor thing. They have these parties, you know. It takes a toll on them. Such a shame!'

MOTHER: Rubbish! Stanley's always here by eight at the latest.

ERROL: Exactly. And he's always back round there by eleven.

MOTHER: Anyway, Errol. It's none of your business. French, blue cheese or mayonnaise dressing, Shelley?

ERROL: She don't know the difference.

MOTHER: Errol!

SHELLEY: Blue cheese, please Miss.

MOTHER: It'll be ready in a minute. We can eat it in here on our knees if you like.

SHELLEY: That's fine, honest. Great.

(MOTHER smiles and goes back in the kitchen.)

ERROL: What is?

SHELLEY: Eating it off our knees.

ERROL: Oh I see. You sound like someone's doing you a favour. *(To MOTHER again.)* Anyway, what did Vernice want?

MOTHER: She's worried about Charmain.

ERROL: She's cracked.

MOTHER: Who is?

ERROL: Charmain, though I suppose both of them might be.

MOTHER: That's not very nice.

ERROL: Neither is Vernice.

MOTHER: You went to middle school with Charmain, didn't you, Shelley?

SHELLEY: Yes, Miss. We were in the same set for nearly everything.

MOTHER: Do you still see her now?

SHELLEY: Well, only about. She's changed a bit.

ERROL: I told you she's cracked. Bloody loony.

MOTHER: Errol, grow up.

SHELLEY: She's sort of gone into herself a bit.

ERROL: Pervert as well.

(MOTHER comes in with three salads on a large tray. She gives ERROL an angry glare.)

MOTHER: It's not very much, Shelley, but I hope it's alright.

SHELLEY: Looks great, Miss. I've never had blue cheese before.

MOTHER: Well, you should have said and I could have given you something else.

SHELLEY: No, it's okay. I wanted to try it anyway.

MOTHER: Well just say if you don't like it.

ERROL: Hey, Shelley. You know it makes you want to…

MOTHER: Errol!

ERROL: Alright. Alright.

SHELLEY: It's nice.

MOTHER: Shall I put the television on whilst you eat?

ERROL: God, no.

MOTHER: But it's the news.

ERROL: Oh, and I suppose that makes it alright.? 'Today sixty-eight youths were sentenced for conspiring to stand on a street corner… All sixty-eight were black.' It's only when you look up that you realise it's a bleeding black newscaster talking. Bloody Uncle Tom.

MOTHER: For heaven's sake, Errol, it's not all like that.

ERROL: Oh yeah.

MOTHER: Well, do you want to listen to some records then? Shelley, perhaps you'd like to put on one of those you brought round for Errol, or perhaps I'll put one of mine on if you like.

SHELLEY: That'd be great, Miss.

ERROL: Oh God. Here we go. Johnny 'oh haven't I been out in the sun a long time' Mathis.

MOTHER: Well, he's not as bad as you.

ERROL: Huh.

(Silence. ERROL is stung.)

SHELLEY: *(To ERROL.)* Laurie Cunningham was on the telly yesterday. Did you see it?

(No answer.)

MOTHER: No I didn't. Was it good?

SHELLEY: Great.

MOTHER: Did you see it, Errol?

ERROL: No.

MOTHER: What's the matter? Have you given up supporting him?

ERROL: I never supported him. You don't support individuals. You support teams.

SHELLEY: Errol supports West Bromwich Albion.

MOTHER: But he doesn't play for them anymore, does he?

ERROL: So what?

SHELLEY: It's alright though for Cyrille Regis and Brendon Batson still do. They're his heroes now.

ERROL: Look, I don't have heroes, right! People who make heroes only have to go through the ritual of breaking them at some point and I can do without that kind of hassle.

MOTHER: What's got into you?

ERROL: Nothing.

MOTHER: Well something's the matter.

ERROL: Nothing's the matter, right? N-O-T-H-I-N-G. Nothing.

MOTHER: We're not stupid, Errol. We can spell.

ERROL: Huh!

MOTHER: And what's that supposed to mean?

ERROL: It's supposed to mean what it sounded like.

MOTHER: I'm not a child, you know. I'm not one of your college friends or your Black Front friends or whatever you call them. You can't go around treating me like dirt and don't you forget it, showing off like a five-year-old.

ERROL: Forget what? Forget what?

MOTHER: I'm in no mind to argue with you.

ERROL: No mind to what? Well?

SHELLEY: I think I'd best be off now and get changed for tonight.

MOTHER: Okay then, Shelley, Errol will see you out.

ERROL: Will he hell. She knows where the door is.

SHELLEY: I'm full up, Miss, but it was great. You don't mind if I leave this bit, do you? *(She stands up.)*

MOTHER: Of course not. Look, I'll just get your umbrella for you.

(MOTHER goes to the kitchen for the umbrella and comes back into the front room.)

SHELLEY: See you at eight, Errol.

(He nods. SHELLEY and MOTHER leave the room and we hear MOTHER let SHELLEY out of the front door. ERROL pokes at his food. MOTHER comes back in.)

MOTHER: I suppose you think that was clever.

ERROL: Think what was clever?

MOTHER: What you've just done.

ERROL: What have I just done?

MOTHER: You know damn well what you've just done. How long do you think you can keep pushing that girl around like that? She's not a toy or a game. She's got feelings

33

too. Well? How long do you think you can keep pushing people around, full stop.

ERROL: I'm not pushing anybody around, and if they think that I am, well, it's their lookout isn't it?

MOTHER: Errol, look at me.

ERROL: I am looking at you.

MOTHER: What's the matter?

ERROL: *(Slams down his plate.)* For Christ's sake, stop asking me that question! There's nothing the matter with me. I'm my own man and if you think that something's wrong with me then it's your lookout. You go ahead and burn yourself up with pointless worry. I'm fine. Doing just fine, thanks. I want to finish my tea in peace.

MOTHER: Doing fine. You must think I'm stupid. Where do you spend the day?

ERROL: None of your business.

MOTHER: I'll tell you where. In that stinking rathole they call a cafe.

ERROL: Who calls it a rathole?

MOTHER: Everyone calls it a rathole.

ERROL: I don't call it a rathole.

MOTHER: You're not everyone and the sooner you wake up to that fact the better. Just look at yourself in the mirror! Do you ever do that? Twenty-one, a second-class degree in Economics from a good college, the world in front of you, and you sit on your arse all day with those jigaboos and drug addicts talking about Africa.

ERROL: Talking about what?

MOTHER: I don't know what you all talk about, but why don't you go and get a job like everyone else?

ERROL: Get a what?

MOTHER: A job for God's sake. Get some order into your life and face up to your responsibilities and reality.

ERROL: What reality do you know about, and what responsibilities have I got, you just tell me that?

MOTHER: For a start you've got a responsibility to me.

ERROL: I've got a responsibility to me, just me, so don't come any of this natural law of obedience crap just because you've got a responsibility to me, and it's tough innit, but that's the Catch-22 of having kids. You're in it up to your neck and you stand or fall by my moral standards. *(Pause.)* I mean, what do you want me to do? Go work for the CRE? Join the police? Stand for Parliament? Or perhaps you want me to make a bid for Trevor McDonald's job and spend the whole day talking shit on the television!

MOTHER: Your reality, Errol, is that girl, and your duty, your responsibility is to look after her, to help her instead of yourself.

ERROL: Utter crap.

MOTHER: Jesus! –

ERROL: – was a white boy and I'm a black boy so don't give me no broken images to worship.

MOTHER: You just tell me what you lazy bastards are doing over and above giving black people a bad name.

ERROL: We're on the march. Africa.

MOTHER: Talk sense, Errol. How the hell are you going to get to Africa, swim? You've got an overdraft the size of the

35

national debt and as long as you sit on your arse talking shit it's going to grow. That's reality. I don't know what kind of economics they taught you, son, but the basics are clear to any fool to see.

ERROL: *(More controlled now.)* What do you know about seeing? Even your own next-door neighbour, who can only just about do subtractions, knows more than you. If my dad was alive he wouldn't take all this crap from you or them sitting down.

MOTHER: How the hell do you know? Come on, tell me how you know he wouldn't take all this 'crap' you say is going around.

ERROL: Because he wouldn't, that's how I know. He's my dad, no man, no black man can stand by and take all this crap.

MOTHER: Errol, listen. What are you talking about? What are you fighting? Tell me, I'd like to know.

ERROL: Tell you shit!

MOTHER: You're driving yourself mad, son. You'll have a breakdown.

ERROL: Have a what?

MOTHER: A breakdown. You're putting too much pressure on yourself.

ERROL: *(Laughs out loud.)* Pressure! I'm putting too much pressure on myself...

MOTHER: Look. Errol, why don't you just have a talk with Alvin tomorrow, eh? If you can't talk to me then for God's sake have a word with your brother. I can't sit by and take this much longer, okay?

36

ERROL: Alvin and I have plans, Mother, that don't include you.

MOTHER: Errol, listen…

ERROL: And when this strike is over we're going to strike again. Yeah, that's it. Two strikes in one by Alvin and Errol Marshall. A study in economic realignment. That's my new black theory of economics that any fool can see, if only they're black enough that is. *(Pause.)* Mother, why don't you put on your Johnny Mathis LP?

(He goes upstairs with the parcel he came in with tucked under his arm. MOTHER just stares at him as he leaves. He doesn't pull the curtain behind him. She is visibly worried. The back door opens and shuts.)

VERNICE: You still home? *(She enters.)* Girl, it must be you going deaf. You not hear me?

MOTHER: Yes, I heard you.

VERNICE: Is it Alvin? Something's happened? What is it?

MOTHER: Nothing. Nothing. What do you want?

VERNICE: Me jus' come round to tell you…

(ERROL comes downstairs in the same clothes, but apparently ready to go out for the night. He has left the parcel upstairs.)

Lord, what make you decide to come back so soon from wherever it is you spend your time?

ERROL: I'm off out.

VERNICE: No sooner you come back as you take up you all backside again. Me ain't know what the hell yer do with you all time.

ERROL: We plan.

VERNICE: Plan, me arse. Only planning you all do is where yerall going get you next spliff from. You still walking out the white girl?

ERROL: Shelley?

VERNICE: Is she who I mean.

ERROL: On and off.

VERNICE: She alright, I suppose. Betta than mosta them. What you think?

ERROL: Scrubber. Boring scrubber at that.

VERNICE: Well look the hell. The boy bad. He swear like a trooper. *(She laughs.)* You better not upset your mother so, you know. Lord. She have enough trouble with you all as it is.

(ERROL sucks his teeth.)

MOTHER: Do you have to go now? I thought you weren't meeting Shelley till eight.

ERROL: I'm walking. After all, we're all going to be walking tomorrow, aren't we?

VERNICE: You just watch yourself, boy, you hear me?

(ERROL smiles at her and goes via the front door.)

Anyhow, Stanley ask me to marry him. That's what me drag meself over here to tell you. When me ring him he jus' ask me straight out on the damn phone when I goin' marry him. You surprise now, ain't you?

MOTHER: And what did you say?

VERNICE: Yes girl, course me goin' marry the man. You don't think me should, or what?

MOTHER: Of course you should, if that's what you want.

VERNICE: Well. I getting on an' I don't think anybody else
　　goin' ask me. Charmain soon goin' leave home an' me
　　can't live on me memories for they all too painful so…
　　So I tell him yes.

MOTHER: I suppose this calls for a drink.

　　(She gets up and goes across to the cabinet. Pause.)

　　Vernice, I'm happy for you.

VERNICE: Me arse. You beginning to sound human.

MOTHER: *(Hands her a drink and sits.)* For you both.

VERNICE: Lord!

　　(They drink.)

MOTHER: Am I the first to know?

VERNICE: Me want to get me hands on Stanley before
　　I going tell anyone else for definite.

MOTHER: That includes Charmain?

VERNICE: Course girl, it includes Charmain.

MOTHER: You mean it's not certain.

VERNICE: Vivien, girl. I know enough men in me time
　　to know that until me feel the ring on this same finger,
　　nothing is definite. I make a fool uh meself enough times
　　over blasted men as it is. Girl, you lucky with having jus'
　　the one man. You ain't waste your time finding out there's
　　no flickin' second chance. Stanley is me last hope.

MOTHER: When will you see him again?

VERNICE: Dinner time is about that time they all crawl
　　round, nuh! *(She laughs.)* Jesus Christ! Why's life so friggin'
　　difficult? Sometimes me feel like jus' packing up me bags

an' goin' home. Pickin' off me mango and drinking me rum. Gimme one drink, huh. *(MOTHER pours her a drink.)* Back home if me feel like doin' me own thing I jus' move me arse an' do it an' don't matter what nobody say they goin' think.

MOTHER: It's different now, though.

VERNICE: Fuck me raas different! What you know about different! In all the years you been here girl, you ain't get off you backside to go down the Caribbean Club, let alone get yerself on a boat or a plane to go and see yer own fockin' family. Girl, you better leave you raas where it is for yer sister Vera goin' cut you good if she done see you comin'.

MOTHER: It's not that I didn't want to…

VERNICE: Bollocks. You didn't want to do this and you didn't want to do that. Lord, you goin' get yer lot when you son come back. And that Errol goin' give the white girl he backfoot an' start taking up with his own. Me see it now. He goin' marry black an' there goin' be plenty trouble.

MOTHER: But Vernice, it doesn't make any difference who he chooses to marry.

VERNICE: Girl, you think too white. *(She helps herself to another drink.)*

MOTHER: What's that supposed to mean? *(VERNICE sucks her teeth.)* Has Charmain got a boyfriend?

VERNICE: Charmain ain't got no boyfriend, girl. She too funny, so and high an' mighty, but when she do I tell you she goin' take up black. Me ain't want no breeds in me family.

MOTHER: Vernice, that's not right.

VERNICE: Lemme tell you. Remember back home at school an' we all use to sit on the beach an' thing an' ask each other if we goin' marry a white man if he ask us, an' how we all say no, we ain't goin' marry no fockin' white. Well today, me arse, them all sitting on they backside asking each other what they goin' do if a black man ask them, and the same with the boys them. What they goin' do if it come they want to marry a black girl.

MOTHER: Rubbish!

VERNICE: Backside, you ain't know the boy. He ain't a child now, you know, and he...

MOTHER: Vernice, do you really wish you were back home?

I mean, would you go tomorrow if you could?

(Pause. They look at each other. VERNICE looks away.)

VERNICE: Me ain't know. I goin' drop off the kettle tomorrow when Stanley bring it round. I hope I goin' find you here you know.

(VERNICE goes via the kitchen. MOTHER, now alone, looks around. She doesn't really want to sit on her own but she has no choice now. She goes back to sit down but is on edge. She gets up and goes into the kitchen for ALVIN's clothes. She comes back through with them, plus an iron. She sets up the ironing board and everything, but can't be bothered to do it just yet. She gets out the photograph album and moves to sit down. She pours herself a drink and opens the album as the lights go down.)

Lights up. It is turned midnight. We hear ERROL and SHELLEY coming in the front door. ERROL comes into the front room first, but is closely followed by SHELLEY. She goes to sit and ERROL throws off his jacket onto the back of the settee. He moves across to go upstairs.

SHELLEY: Where you off?

ERROL: I'm off for a piss, you wanna come?

SHELLEY: No, I just wondered, that's all.

> *(ERROL goes. SHELLEY takes off her coat and sees to her face in the mirror. She hears him coming back so she quickly rushes back to her seat as if she hasn't moved. ERROL comes in and shuts the door, pulling the curtain across it.)*

She isn't awake, is she?

ERROL: Who?

> *(He goes to the cabinet, deciding what drink to have.)*

SHELLEY: You know who. Your mum.

ERROL: Don't know. What d'you wanna drink?

SHELLEY: Anything really, I'm not bothered. *(Pause.)* What is there?

ERROL: You asked for 'anything really' so that's what you've got now.

> *(He hands her a drink.)*

SHELLEY: Thanks. Cheers.

> *(ERROL sucks his teeth.)*

I see she finished off Alvin's stuff before she went to bed.

ERROL: Shit. She did 'n' all.

42

(He goes to the pile of ironed clothes in the corner.)

SHELLEY: I feel sorry for her.

ERROL: *(Picking it up.)* See this dashiki?

SHELLEY: This what?

ERROL: This shirt.

SHELLEY: Yeah.

ERROL: Alvin's gonna give it to me when he gets back 'cos he's buying one out there. He's gonna bring us some beads too.

SHELLEY: That'd be nice.

ERROL: What?

SHELLEY: I said that'd be nice.

ERROL: *(Mimicking.)* 'That'd be nice.' Have you seen his shades?

SHELLEY: No, I don't think so.

ERROL: No, you wouldn't have I don't suppose. Do you wanna?

SHELLEY: If you like.

ERROL: Here. He keeps them in here in the back of this drawer.

(He finds them and puts them on.)

SHELLEY: Is that 'em?

ERROL: No, it's a packet of Tampax I've got strapped to me head or didn't you notice?

SHELLEY: I've never seen him wearing them so how am I supposed to know that they're the ones? Anyhow, I've seen some like them before. Did he get 'em from Woolies?

43

ERROL: Woolies? You've never seen anyone wearing these, or any like 'em. These specs aren't for wearing. He got 'em off a Black American GI who knew Huey Newton. They're Huey Newton's dark glasses. Genuine Panther specs.

SHELLEY: Really? You mean Black Panthers have worn them?

ERROL: I just said so, didn't I?

SHELLEY: I know, but I'd never have believed it just to look at them.

ERROL: You what? *(He puts them away sharply.)* You don't know what the fuck you're on about half the time, do you? Well answer me. Do you?

(She looks like she is going to start crying.)

Oh for fuck's sake, I might as well talk to the wall.

(He goes for another drink.)

SHELLEY: Sorry.

ERROL: What you sorry for?

SHELLEY: I don't know. I'm just sorry, that's all.

ERROL: Jesus!

(Long pause.)

SHELLEY: Errol.

ERROL: Yeah, that's me. I'm still here remember?

SHELLEY: I think…

ERROL: Well, go on then. Quit the Hitchcock suspense stuff, will you?

SHELLEY: I think I'm going to have to leave home after my exams.

44

ERROL: So?

SHELLEY: You can't just say 'so', it's important.

ERROL: Okay then. For fuck's sake, why have you got to leave home?

SHELLEY: I don't know.

ERROL: Brilliant. Well, what do you want me to do? Go and ask the FBI to investigate, because I've got a hotline to J. Edgar Hoover upstairs if you're interested. I'll just go give him a buzz shall I?

(He moves to go upstairs.)

SHELLEY: But it's serious.

ERROL: Course it's serious. It's so fucking serious you don't know what the hell you're on about. You might have to leave home but you don't know why! You must think I'm a fucking idiot. Well? Simple really, isn't it. Your wonderful parents can't handle the idea of their virginal lily-white maiden possibly falling prey to the lascivious clutches of an old black ram. *Othello*, page sixty-one or whatever. Well? Come on. They remember when this area was Cortina-country. You know, all kippers and curtains or whatever, don't they?

SHELLEY: He's a motherfucker.

ERROL: Who's a motherfucker? Othello? I think you've got the wrong classical 'O' there. No doubt you'll find Oedipus is your man, if you bothered to pay any attention to what people tell you instead of daydreaming your way through life.

SHELLEY: My dad. He's a motherfucker.

ERROL: Your dad?

45

SHELLEY: Yes.

ERROL: *(Laughs.)* Look, you can't call your dad a motherfucker.

SHELLEY: Why not? You say it.

ERROL: 'Cos your dad is a motherfucker. That's why you're here, right, brain of Britain. Jesus. *(Takes it slowly.)* In theory he has at some point fucked your mother, i.e. motherfucker.

SHELLEY: I'm sorry.

ERROL: What you sorry about now? Well?

SHELLEY: I don't know.

ERROL: Oh, I see, you don't know again. Shall I change the record?

SHELLEY: I'm sorry about calling my dad a motherfucker.

ERROL: Oh, I see. I think a 'mindless ugly little redneck bastard' would be a fairer description. Well? Is that all?

SHELLEY: I don't know where I'm going to.

ERROL: You could enrol at Madame Sheila's on Rose Street as a hostess. Give us a massage from time to time.

SHELLEY: Is that all you think of me? Is that all you think I'm worth?

ERROL: Oh bollocks. I was only kidding.

SHELLEY: Well, it's not funny. I don't think it's funny at all.

ERROL: Alright I'm sorry. What do you want? Some kind of twenty-one-gun salute 'cos your redneck fucking old man's kicking you out?

(He goes for a drink.)

SHELLEY: I've been thinking...

ERROL: Go on. I'm intrigued.

SHELLEY: Well, maybe we could get a place and...

ERROL: Now I'm amused.

SHELLEY: Why?

ERROL: Oh, come off it.

SHELLEY: It's over two years now, Errol. What do you want from me? I've got feelings too, you know. You can't just go on treating me like dirt.

ERROL: Who's treating you like dirt?

SHELLEY: You are. You never take any notice of anything I say. I might as well not bother, I might as well blend into the wallpaper for all you care. Don't you love me anymore?

ERROL: Don't I what?

SHELLEY: Don't you love me anymore? Have you gone off me?

ERROL: When did I say I loved you?

SHELLEY: Errol!

ERROL: Well, that was ages ago and...

SHELLEY: For a girl it's never ages ago, it's always in her mind. *(Pause.)* I only let you because you...

ERROL: ...Bollocks!

SHELLEY: I did! You said that you'd never felt like this before and it was special and...

ERROL: *(Stands.)* Fucking hell! I must have had a few beers.

47

SHELLEY: Errol, you can't just leave me now, you know. You can't just ditch me like that. You've got responsibility. You owe me something.

ERROL: Owe you what? I owe you shit.

SHELLEY: How can you say that, Errol? After everything I've put up with. After I get used to being just a source of amusement for you and your spars, or whatever you call them. Just a good joke. After I get used to you not talking to me, and when you do it's just to tell me how stupid I am. After I even get used to you screwing those fourth-formers round the back of the club. Yeah, you thought I didn't know, but I'm not stupid, I'm not as stupid as all that and it's them that belong down Rose Street, not me. You owe me something. You've got to look after me, Errol. Please, you've got to look after me.

ERROL: I've got my own plans and they don't include you.

SHELLEY: But they must. They have to...

ERROL: Why? You think you're special, don't you? You think you're somebody really special don't you, just 'cos I've been knocking about with you for a bit.

SHELLEY: Doesn't it mean something to you? After two years it must do, Errol.

ERROL: Yeah. It means you're probably a good screw, which as a matter of fact you aren't. You're just regular, that's all.

SHELLEY: What, you mean just when you need me.

ERROL: That's right.

SHELLEY: A quick one in the bog at the club, or round here when your mum's at work.

ERROL: Don't forget the shop doorways. You were always at your best standing up.

SHELLEY: And that's all I am to you.

ERROL: If you put it like that.

SHELLEY: You're a bastard sometimes.

ERROL: Oh piss off, woman.

SHELLEY: I don't deserve this, Errol, I deserve better.

ERROL: Don't make me laugh, pasty-face. Only two parts
of a man's body a woman understands, and if you don't
shut up I'm gonna belt your fucking face in with this,
understand, my number-two weapon. *(He clenches his fist
and there is a long pause.)*

SHELLEY: Don't you have any respect left for me?

ERROL: Shall I tell you what you and others like you deserve?
Shall I tell you what you are? You're finished. You thought
you could push us around, didn't you? Didn't you?

SHELLEY: I don't understand, Errol.

(Throughout the speech he challenges her both vocally and physically.)

ERROL: There's a phrase. Malcolm used it: 'Chickens coming
home to roost.'

SHELLEY: Errol.

ERROL: In your case it means you don't control shit anymore.
You don't control the land, the money or the mind. Now
you're the tool and we're the craftsmen. Look around the
world. Suddenly you're all frightened. There are more
black Prime Ministers than white ones. There are more
black people than white people. You're a minority – a
sickening minority at that. Your economy is all to fuck so
what do you do? You try and kick out those of us who are
already here and stop anyone else from coming in. Well,
it ain't fucking working, is it? We're a beautiful people, a

talented, resourceful, strong, dark people, a people just waking up. We're growing and you're scared shitless. Look at yourselves. You need us, you bastards. You need to control us. We've wheedled our way into the main artery of your fucked-up economic system. You can't kick us out like Hitler did to the Jews 'cos if you want to play at being Nazis we ain't your fuckin' jewboys. In the next two days you and others like you will see what you really are. To you all reality is just a game, but to us it's fucking survival, it's pressure, and what fucking pressure do you all know, sticking your ugly heads in the sand? We're gonna show you some reality. Let's see you hold down some pressure. You're so fucking short-sighted you make me laugh. We are here because you were there. The chickens are coming home to roost. That's all you are to me – a historical phenomenon.

(He begins to strut around, squawking – he's doing the 'funky chicken'. He repeats the last sentence, taunting her with it. She just watches him helplessly. After a few moments MOTHER comes downstairs and looks on. She has got out of bed. She wears her dressing gown and slippers.)

Oh hello, mother. We're just playing. Honest, that's all.

(He carries on.)

MOTHER: I don't know what the hell kind of playing you call this, but I thought you'd left all that kind of nonsense behind with the train sets and cowboys and Indians. Why don't you grow up?

ERROL: *(Stops.)* What for?

MOTHER: Shelley, are you alright dear?

SHELLEY: Yes, Miss.

ERROL: Why don't you call her Mrs Marshall, or Ma'am, or God or something? 'Yes, Miss!'

MOTHER: Have you been drinking, Errol?

ERROL: Camels don't need to drink to get high. They just stand up.

MOTHER: Look, it's getting on Errol, and I've got to…

ERROL: Yeah, go on.

MOTHER: I've got to get some sleep. Shelley, as it's late you can sleep here on the settee if you like. Give your parents a ring and tell them if you decide you want to.

SHELLEY: It'll be alright thanks, but I'll have to get back 'cos I've got school tomorrow.

ERROL: Yeah, what a drag. We're having a quiet day in. Some kind of strike or summat on. Don't know if you've heard about it?

MOTHER: Well, I don't mind if you put on some records or something but please try to keep the noise down. People are trying to sleep.

SHELLEY: We're sorry.

MOTHER: It's okay, Shelley.

ERROL: It's okay, Shelley. It's my tits she's getting on.

MOTHER: Goodnight, and don't forget to lock up behind you when you come up.

(She goes.)

ERROL: Goodnight.

SHELLEY: Please, Errol. You should treat her better. She's your mother.

ERROL: I wondered who it was standing there. I knew I'd seen her somewhere. *(Pause.)* Oh, come off it, Shelley. Let's forget it, eh love?

SHELLEY: Forget what?

ERROL: You know. Argument and everything. I'm just playing.

SHELLEY: But Errol.

ERROL: But Errol, nothing. You fancy a cup of tea?

SHELLEY: Yeah, okay.

ERROL: Okay, I'll get it.

(He gets up and goes into the kitchen.)

SHELLEY: Do you want a hand?

ERROL: No. I've just got to put the water in the pan, that's all. Bloody kettle's knackered. It won't be a minute.

SHELLEY: Can't you fix it?

ERROL: Fix what?

SHELLEY: The kettle.

ERROL: Fix it!

SHELLEY: Well, I thought you might be able to adjust something.

ERROL: *(Comes through.)* I'm an Economist and Revolutionary. What the fuck am I supposed to know about electric kettles?

SHELLEY: Nothing, I suppose.

ERROL: Well, there you are then.

SHELLEY: Errol?

ERROL: What now? You want me to fix in some double glazing for you, or maybe you think I ought to refit the carpet whilst the kettle's boiling?

SHELLEY: No. What I wanted to say was, what do you want to do?

ERROL: What kind of question is that?

SHELLEY: Well, what's your ambition, you know? Your goal.

ERROL: I don't have ambition or goal. I have destiny.

SHELLEY: Well, it's the same thing, isn't it?

ERROL: In a word, no.

SHELLEY: What is it, then?

ERROL: Hang on.

(He goes back into kitchen.)

I'm having a Red Stripe.

SHELLEY: Can I have one too?

ERROL: You said you wanted tea.

SHELLEY: I'll have both. It'll help to calm me down.

ERROL: Or loosen up, more like. One cup of tea and a Red Stripe coming up.

(He comes through.)

SHELLEY: Thanks, Errol.

ERROL: Not at all, Miss.

SHELLEY: Can I put an album on? One of those I brought round for you to play?

ERROL: Let's have a look at them first.

53

SHELLEY: You won't like them.

ERROL: Well, what the fuck did you bring them round for?

SHELLEY: I thought we might listen to them.

ERROL: Even though I don't like them. Well? *(He sucks his teeth.)* You don't listen to the fuckin' lyrics, anyway.

SHELLEY: Well, I…

ERROL: Let's have a look at them.

(SHELLEY gets them.)

Oh my God! I might have guessed. These fuckin' mixed bands are a disgrace! It's only one step better yet they're all too fucking stupid to realise it. What we want is black bands. Black producers and arrangers and black singers to do their own thing. Black businessmen means black music.

SHELLEY: But there isn't any Tamla Motown in England, so how are you going to get all of these things.

ERROL: There's Eddy Grant.

SHELLEY: Who?

ERROL: He does it on his own. He does it all. He lives on the frontline and he's a…he's a…

SHELLEY: He's a what?

ERROL: He runs his own show – does his own thing – entrepreneur. Black entrepreneur. Uses black capital like Berry Gordy.

SHELLEY: I've never heard of him.

ERROL: He's an example, that's what he is. An example of something. *(Pause.)* Take them away and come back here next to me.

(She gets up and puts the albums back. She comes and sits down next to him again.)

My destiny is that of a leader. A leader, do you understand?

SHELLEY: Yeah, I know. I thought that's what you wanted to be. You can do it you know, Errol. *(Pause.)* You're always saying your destiny's to be free, aren't you?

ERROL: The promised land. Freedom of spirit and mind. Freedom of body and action. Do you understand?

SHELLEY: I understand. I see. *(Pause.)* Why don't you kiss me, Errol, if it makes you feel free?

ERROL: Alvin too. Co-leaders. Tomorrow there'll be a Patriotic Front in Britain.

SHELLEY: Hold me, Errol.

ERROL: Tomorrow the sun comes up on a sunken kingdom. An Empire in ruins.

SHELLEY: Don't leave me, Errol. Please.

ERROL: An Empire that's fallen. In the whole history of the world there is no Empire, not even the Roman Empire, that has not come crashing down.

SHELLEY: Errol.

ERROL: And do you know what brought them down – all of them?

SHELLEY: Please Errol.

ERROL: The lust for freedom.

SHELLEY: Please.

ERROL: No man has been more systematically denied his freedom than the black man. Our day is coming. The seeds will soon be plants and the plants will begin to bear forth fruit. *(He turns to SHELLEY.)* And you, all of you, did the sowing.

SHELLEY: Errol, love me.

ERROL: Take them off.

SHELLEY: Yes.

(She begins to take off her tights and pants.)

ERROL: Quick. *(He begins to fumble at his jeans. They begin to make love on the settee.)*

SHELLEY: Errol, Errol.

ERROL: Faster. You sowed, now work, work, work!

SHELLEY: Oh, Errol, this is your destiny. I'm doing it for you, it's for you, just for you.

ERROL: Oh fuck. Fuck, oh, oh! *(He reaches a climax, whilst she still wants more as he does so. After the stillness he comes through and she still wants more. He pushes her off and zips up.)* You'd better go now.

SHELLEY: Errol!

ERROL: It's getting late and you've got to go to school tomorrow, remember.

SHELLEY: You can't. Not again, Errol. Not again.

ERROL: Look, it's late, okay. *(She begins to cry as he picks up the phone and starts to dial for a taxi.)* Can I have a cab please at 201 Crawley Terrace…yes…to Elm Park Estate…just one…five minutes, okay. It'll be here in five minutes.

(Long pause.)

SHELLEY: Errol, I know where my dad's got some money hidden. We could be leaders together, direct our own destiny if that's what you want.

ERROL: What the fuck is this? I don't believe it. You're trying to buy me now.

SHELLEY: I'm not, Errol.

ERROL: How much do you think I cost, then? Three necklaces and a string of plastic beads? Or perhaps just a piece of shiny glass.

SHELLEY: He's got about five hundred pounds under his bed. He doesn't trust banks and I know I can get it while he's out and then we can…

ERROL: I know. We can get ourselves set up in a flat when you get chucked out for insisting on fucking with a nigger. Well?

SHELLEY: We could go away.

ERROL: Where to?

SHELLEY: Couldn't I come to Africa with you?

ERROL: Do me a favour. I don't need no fucking white woman to dangle on a string to show I'm free. I don't need no colour television or white sports car either. When I get off that plane in Africa, you know what I'm gonna do? I'm gonna walk barefoot down the steps onto the tarmac, and kiss the ground like that white cunt, the Pope. I'm gonna sit out in the sun all day listening to the drums till I'm as black as coal. I'm gonna sit there and feel fine 'cos everywhere I turn they'll be as black as me. I'll find myself a family, a new family. Can't I take you to Africa with me! Put your fucking clothes on and watch you don't mess up the woman's settee, you raas clart.

57

(He pours himself a drink as SHELLEY starts to put on her tights and pants. There is a noticeable lull then SHELLEY speaks up.)

SHELLEY: Is it all over then, Errol? Is that what you're trying to tell me because…

ERROL: Woman, don't ask me such fockin' damn fool questions. Jus' put on yer clothes, nuh. The man goin' come at any moment.

SHELLEY: Can I see you tomorrow afternoon?

ERROL: *(Sucks his teeth.)* Me got me plans to sort out with Alvin.

SHELLEY: But I need to see you tomorrow afternoon.

(Sound of car horn.)

ERROL: You ain't needing nothing but one good bath.

SHELLEY: I want to see you tomorrow, please. Please.

ERROL: Girl, you keeping the man waiting.

SHELLEY: Please, Errol. Please.

(She starts to get hysterical. ERROL puts down his drink and hits her across the face.)

ERROL: You going wake up the focking woman again, you hear me. Get your focking records and go.

(SHELLEY crosses and picks them up. She stares at him then moves towards the door. She has a last desperate attempt. She turns.)

Go! And shut the door behind your arse, nuh, raas!

(The car horn sounds again. SHELLEY leaves. ERROL is on edge. He pours a drink down himself.)

(Lights down.)

END OF ACT ONE

Act Two

SCENE ONE

Lights up. Tuesday: 6.30 a.m.

MOTHER comes downstairs in her dressing gown and slippers. She is carrying an alarm clock, which she places on the sideboard. She picks up her sewing basket and some of ALVIN's clothes. She turns on the fire and sits in front of it all huddled up, cold and shivering. Wearily she begins to sew. After a minute or so we hear a light tapping on the kitchen window. At first she is startled, then she realises who it must be. She puts down her work and goes into the kitchen.

MOTHER: Do you know what time it is?

VERNICE: Yes, girl, but I couldn't sleep.

(They enter the front room. VERNICE has on her dressing gown and slippers too.)

MOTHER: Keep it quiet or you'll wake up Errol...

VERNICE: I see you light on so me think me goin' call round an' see if y'alright.

MOTHER: I couldn't sleep.

VERNICE: Neither could I.

MOTHER: I kept hearing noises like...

VERNICE: Like what?

MOTHER: Like drums in the night.

VERNICE: *(Sucks her teeth.)* That be nothin', girl. It jus' be Errol talking to him brothers in Africa. *(She laughs.)*

MOTHER: I was scared, though.

VERNICE: *(Sucks her teeth.)* Fear's the least uh yer problems.

MOTHER: I wish they'd go to church.

VERNICE: Who?

MOTHER: My two.

VERNICE: You make me laugh. To get them kids into church, you must be joking.

MOTHER: Errol told me it's a white man's institution because it deals with the hereafter instead of the now on earth. Only poor people go to church, so he claims.

VERNICE: You ask the boy when he did win the pools. He think he rich or something. Girl, we needed the church then.

MOTHER: I still need it, and I haven't noticed you queuing up for a seat.

VERNICE: Girl, back home we didn't know nothing else, and when we first come here I don't have to tell you where the only place you feel safe is.

MOTHER: No, you don't have to tell me.

VERNICE: Girl, everywhere we turn. 'No coloureds here' an' 'No vacancies for coloureds'. And the kids them callin' at we in the street. 'Nigger whore, fuck off home' an' 'Monkey, monkey show us your tail'. You remember?

MOTHER: Vernice.

VERNICE: You want to ask that boy of yours how he think a coloured woman arriving in this fockin' country with jus' she two children an' no father for them is goin' get along without the church. *(Pause.)* Life's jus' like one long, long journey and you jus' gotta keep jumping up an' over the obstacles, you hear me? Birth, marriage, death

60

of parents, death of friends, divorce, death of husbands, grandchildren you never goin' see, but you jus' gotta keep on jumpin' otherwise you goin' fall flat on you all face.

MOTHER: I'm sick and tired of jumping.

VERNICE: Well, get out the house, nuh, and find yourself somebody.

MOTHER: I've managed so far.

VERNICE: Well, if you don't want to be carried you've got to talk to someone. *(Pause.)* If it wasn't Wilfred it was somebody, girl. Jus' somebody to help me survive. *(Pause.)* Lord, me ain't know how you do it. I thief money for Charmain's uniform and me still fiddling on the social security yet me still poor. Lord, me ain't know what me goin' do if they find out.

(Pause.)

MOTHER: The first time I ever saw snow in England, Vernice. The first time. Have I ever told you?

VERNICE: Jesus!

MOTHER: I remember. I'd just applied for a job as a clerk with the buses. I'd given up the job in the shoe factory. 'My name is Mrs Marshall, not black sambo, my name is Mrs Marshall, not black sambo, my name is…' and so on. Normal factory job. Alvin was at school. Mrs Teale's class. Errol had whooping cough. I had no money and you and Wilfred had taken Charmain to Bradford to see Wilfred's brother, I think it was. Just before he died. I was alone, as usual, and it was the night before the interview for the clerk's job. I broke into the meter with a nail file. It took me six hours in the dark. All night I filed away as the mice ran about my feet looking for bits of food. Anything at all, scrambling behind the cooker and in the dustbin, in

61

the bottom of the cupboard, and God knows how, even
on the table top itself. I guess they were hungry too, but
Alvin had beaten them to it. He'd been through all those
places long before they had. It was still dark as the lock
eventually gave way and I pulled out the tray. I pushed
a sixpence back into the meter, turned the dial, and then
discovered that the mice were rats and that there were
only three sixpences left in the tray. Four, when I picked
up the one I'd just put in off the floor. My life savings
amounted to two shillings, and it was stolen money at
that. They said the interview was to be at nine o'clock at
the main depot, so I had four hours to go. I turned out the
lights and sat in the dark again. Then I realised it didn't
matter about saving electricity, for the money just came
back to me and I could put it back in again and so on, so I
put the lights back on. Errol began to cry so I brought him
down and lay him in front of the paraffin heater, hoping
that the fumes would help him sleep. I didn't realise
that they just made his cough worse. The doctor didn't
mention anything about that. When Alvin got up I left the
pair of them and went out to buy some breakfast. I spent
a shilling. I needed a sixpence for the meter and sixpence
for my bus fare to the depot. I'd hoped I'd start that
morning so I didn't leave any change for the return fare.
After they'd eaten, Alvin left for school and I took Errol to
the nursery and told them it was just a bad cough and as
long as they kept him away from the other kids it would
be alright. Well, what else could I do? I needed the job
and only then would I be able to get a proper minder. It
was half past eight. I'd get to the depot just in time. It was
full downstairs so I went upstairs, fighting my way through
the smoke and flat caps till I got to the front. I could feel
the comments and hatred behind me, taste their grimy,
filthy lusting. As we neared the factory gates they all began
to get up and move down the bus. As they did so one of
them began to sing 'Bye, bye, Blackbird' and soon they

were all singing it. I closed my already heavy and swollen eyes and tried to fight back the tears. It wasn't really much good, was it? There's no such thing as getting used to it. If there's one thing I know it's that. I didn't even bother to wipe them away. Perhaps if they saw tears they'd realise I was human. Perhaps not. 'Come on, love. You're just soft. Can't you take a joke?' I shut my eyes even tighter, then I felt a hand on my shoulder. 'Terminus. That'll be fourpence extra. You only paid a tanner.' I opened my eyes. 'Where are we?' I asked. 'Don't you speak English? Terminus. Great Hayton Park. Don't know what you're doing up here.' 'Have I passed the depot?' He sneered at me, then I realised what had happened. I'd fallen asleep and missed the stop. Missed the appointment. I'd just have to be late. 'I'm going back to the depot,' I said. 'Where's your brass then? That'll be eightpence.' I had no money. In that split second of panic I decided to explain. I looked up at him. Sensitive? A sensitive man? Does his daughter play with Alvin at school? Will his grandson marry my granddaughter? 'Get off the bus, nigger, and walk. I'm not taking any of you liver-lipped lot, whether you've got the money or not. Well, move on or there'll be another Notting Hill riot right here.' Did his grandfather own my grandfather? I began to walk but the houses all looked so big, they all looked the same and all the streets even seemed to have the same cars parked on them. The same little dogs played in the garden and the same hands pulled the children back from the gate as I passed. I'd walked in a circle. I was lost. I opened a gate and knocked at a door. I saw the curtain move but I had to ask. A woman of my age opened the door except she was white. 'Excuse me please, but which is the way back to town, please?' No answer. 'Excuse me please?' She spat in my face and my stomach rushed into my mouth as I was sick. She screamed and a man ran out and punched me in the face. He dragged me out of the gate, onto the pavement, and threw me onto the grass verge. I continued to be sick. No food, just bile. Green and white slime. Then it began to snow. I'd never seen snow before but I'd always thought that when it did snow – when I did get to England and see snow – it would be the happiest moment of my life. Nature's most beautiful costume and I'd never seen it. I wet my pants and shivered.

(Long pause.)

VERNICE: Lord, you ain't tell me this before, Vivien.

MOTHER: I don't know. It's not important.

(She gets up and goes to pour herself a drink.)

VERNICE: *(Sucks her teeth.)* You'd come to the wrong country.

MOTHER: No. Not me. I was on the right island. I'd been reading the wrong books. Listening to lies.

VERNICE: It was the truth, then, you know. Back home.

MOTHER: I don't know what they want. Blood?

VERNICE: Who?

MOTHER: Everybody. All of them. My children.

VERNICE: Charmain's already had mine. If Stanley don't say he goin' marry me she only goin' have the bones left to chew.

MOTHER: Don't you ever feel like you're losing touch?

VERNICE: Lord, sometimes me feel like me ain't ever been in touch to start with. Me better go an' see if the girl's alright.

MOTHER: I'll see you later. *(VERNICE gets up.)* Vernice?

VERNICE: Girl, I hear you. You better put away that rum, you hear.

64

(She goes, leaving MOTHER alone for a few moments. The alarm clock goes off. She gets up and switches it off, then hesitates. She picks it up and goes upstairs to get dressed.)

(Lights down.)

SCENE TWO

Lights up. Early afternoon of the same day.

ERROL comes downstairs carrying a cardboard box of what looks like papers and assorted rubbish. His hair is still uncombed and he has nothing on his feet. His shoes and socks are in the box. He turns on the radio for a time-check, then goes into the kitchen to see if MOTHER is there. He comes out. The radio says it's one o'clock. He turns it off because it's news time. He goes into the kitchen and we hear him putting on the pan for some water to boil up. He comes back into the room and sits. He puts on his shoes and socks. He checks that SHELLEY didn't make a mess on the settee last night by rubbing his hand over it and smelling it. Nothing, so he licks it. Then he starts to take the stuff out of the box. He unfolds a huge sheet of folded paper and we see it has on it drawings of roads. He puts it on the floor, having made enough room for it by pushing back the settee a little. The sheet of paper is a ground plan, which also has arrows and stickers on it. Onto the plan he places cardboard cut-outs of buildings, which he takes from the box. He completes the design with strategically placed toy cars. He gets out a pencil and draws a few arrows, only to rub them out and think. The water's boiling, so he goes through and comes back with a cup of coffee. He's just settling down to work again when he hears VERNICE calling out. He scrambles to get everything back into the box and pushes it under the settee. Enter VERNICE, carrying a kettle.

VERNICE: Morning!

ERROL: It's afternoon.

VERNICE: *(Sucks her teeth.)* After one, for your information.

65

ERROL: I know.

VERNICE: Well, ain't you got 'morning' in your dictionary?

ERROL: Afternoon.

VERNICE: You jus' get up?

ERROL: No… Yeah.

VERNICE: No, yeah, me arse. Boy you look rough. You out with the white girl, shufflin' your foot last night?

ERROL: Yeah.

VERNICE: All you all don't know how to move yer arse any more Lord, back home we move so. Even you all mother move sheself. *(She demonstrates.)*

ERROL: Well, it was easy for you lot. All you had to do was listen to the bongos, wasn't it? What's that for?

VERNICE: Come again?

ERROL: That?

VERNICE: Oh, this you talking about? You put it under you bed at night to pee in if you all too lazy to get outa bed, what you think it for? Boy, it's a kettle.

ERROL: Yeah, alright, I know it's a kettle, but what's it doing here? Is it for us?

VERNICE: Me ring up Stanley yesterday and ask him if he can bring me round a spare kettle for me remember long time ago he say he have one. He bring me this ordinary cooker kettle around an' telling me it better than electric kettle for it work on gas too. *(Sucks her teeth.)*

ERROL: He's a prat.

VERNICE: Anyhow, here it is. I goin' make meself a quick cuppa with it.

(She goes into the kitchen. ERROL pushes the box further out of sight.)

ERROL: Vernice.

VERNICE: Me hear you.

ERROL: How come he's working today?

VERNICE: Well, he has to, otherwise he'll lose his customers and his round. Or so the man tell me when he drop off the kettle, an' it make a bita sense me suppose.

ERROL: But that's the whole point. To show them that we don't need them. We don't care. They need us.

VERNICE: *(Coming back through.)* But Stanley's already essential. He knows that.

ERROL: Essential to who?

VERNICE: To everyone in the area. The community.

ERROL: What if everyone decided to do that, eh? What about me mother? You could say the same for her 'n' all couldn't you, but you don't.

VERNICE: Child, don't vex me up so. Is you who always talking about serve the community and serve that so here is a big chance to do some serving on your own doorstep.

ERROL: I talk about serving a people, not a community.

VERNICE: I don't care who the hell you talking about serving, but why the hell you not come round and help Charmain? According to your mother she ain't doing the work.

ERROL: Well, you know why she don't do any work, don't you? It's 'cos she spends half the day wandering the streets and sitting in the park. She isn't stupid.

VERNICE: She doesn't know anything about Stanley.

ERROL: Don't be stupid. Course she does.

VERNICE: Know what?

ERROL: Everything. Why don't you just come out into the open with it? It'd probably be the best thing.

VERNICE: You really think so…?

ERROL: Course. Just tell her.

VERNICE: I was going to today but now he's…

ERROL: Now he's what?

VERNICE: Nothing much. I'll ring him tonight.

ERROL: It's truth not tuition that we need, Vernice.

VERNICE: Someone at the door, nuh?

ERROL: Shit, it's probably Alvin.

VERNICE: What, so soon? I thought your mother say he ain't coming till after three.

ERROL: Well, that's what I thought but…

(Enter ALVIN with a large suitcase and a large flight bag. He is twenty-four, slim and slightly taller than ERROL; casually but tidily dressed, with his hair cut closely but neatly. He wears a gold signet ring on his right hand and a thin gold chain around his neck, visible because of his open collar. He is too casual to be important, yet too smart to be bullied in the streets by the police – at least on a first glance.)

Hey man, what's happening?

ALVIN: Hey man, what's happening with you!

ERROL: Alright, the prodigal son!

(They slap hands, US fashion.)

VERNICE: *(Comes through with her drink.)* Well, look the hell. Son of Africa decide to come home.

ALVIN: How you doing, Vernice?

VERNICE: Me fine, but how come you get back so damn quick? I hope you ain't catch no bus nor train for this one goin' give you some licks if you break up the strike.

ERROL: We have ways of making you walk!

ALVIN: No, I met someone on the plane who gave me a lift from the airport. Drove a Scimitar.

VERNICE: A what?

ALVIN: Scimitar. You know, Reliant. Sports car.

VERNICE: Me jus' hope the man black. *(Sucks her teeth.)* You want tea?

ALVIN: Yeah. That'd be great, thanks.

(She goes into the kitchen.) How you doing, man?

ERROL: I-rey. I-rey.

ALVIN: Alright.

ERROL: Jesus, man. We weren't expecting you for at least another hour or so.

ALVIN: Complaining?

ERROL: No, course not. Just great. Great.

ALVIN: *(Inspecting the place.)* That's the way it is. *(Pause.)* Christ, man. Nothing much changes around here, does it?

ERROL: Raas man. Babylon will fall, give it time, me brother. All I and I need is a little time fe we survive.

69

VERNICE: *(Coming back with a cup of tea.)* Boy, what happen to all you hair, nuh?

ERROL: Yeah. What happened?

ALVIN: What do you mean, what happened?

VERNICE: Look the hell! What happened, nuh? *(She sits down.)*

ERROL: You come a baldhead, nuh. And all this gold and thing. I thought you throw them away. You never use to wear them before.

ALVIN: Well...

VERNICE: Well what, me arse. The boy gone an' find himself some pretty black girl with plenty money. Is right?

ERROL: Hey!

ALVIN: Come on. I just wanted to get it cut for the funeral and everything.

VERNICE: Boy, you pants tight so it looks like something goin' give way. Is how they wearing things now?

ALVIN: I suppose so. I don't really know.

ERROL: Hey, have you got jet lag? What's it like?

ALVIN: Yeah. I'm a bit knackered.

VERNICE: Ain't no aeroplane finish the boy off, I tell you. He been spending too much time messin' up the girls them.

ERROL: Yeah, I bet.

VERNICE: Boy, you looking good, though. You raas clart man, you looking fine you know. You might even say that for once you got you all black backside looking respectable.

ALVIN: *(Sarcastic.)* Why, I thank you both. Nice of you to say so.

(VERNICE sucks her teeth.)

ERROL: Raas!

(They slap hands again.)

VERNICE: How all you family then? You get on with them?

ALVIN: Sort of.

ERROL: What d'you mean, sort of?

ALVIN: Well, they're a funny lot, you know.

VERNICE: Boy, I hope you ain't come none uh that college shit with you people, for they goin' think you come jus' like you all mother.

ALVIN: Nothing like that.

ERROL: You bet. You probably told them there were elephants in Piccadilly Circus.

ALVIN: Don't be a prick.

VERNICE: No ain't know why the pair of you bother doing any studying for if all you going do is play the arse, nuh.

ERROL: We're studying our own thing now, Vernice. He's got his own brand of politics and I've got my own brand of economics. Boy, what a team! What a team!

VERNICE: What you goin' win?

ERROL: Win?

VERNICE: Why you not get your arse across and teach me child 'steada playing the arse.

ALVIN: Charmain?

ERROL: Flunking out at school.

VERNICE: What you say?

ERROL: Flunking.

VERNICE: Boy, me hope that ain't rude, for if it is I goin' thump you arse one lick.

ALVIN: No, Vernice. It means not doing too well.

ERROL: That's right.

VERNICE: Well, why you not say that?

ERROL: I did in a different way.

VERNICE: You all fockin' education an' the girl strugglin' so. Look, I goin' now but I hope I goin' see you all an' you schoolbooks later on, save me some time an' some friggin' money. *(To ALVIN.)* And I hope you ain't mash up me camera. I expect to see it later on too.

(She exits.)

ERROL: Things getting organised you know, man. They coming together and there be a lotta plans and things we gotta get sorted out if we going link up with the strike an' everything. For a few days me didn't think you going make it back in time, man. I shitting up meself, but then me remember you have you flight book up and everything. Still, plans man, plans.

ALVIN: Hey, hold on, man.

ERROL: What?

ALVIN: Well, just hold it, that's all. You've got to at least give us some time to do some eating and a bit of thinking. God, I'm knackered out, you know.

(ERROL gets up and goes through to the kitchen.)

ERROL: Suppose you used to rice and goat now.

ALVIN: What?

72

ERROL: Rice and goat. Ram goat liver and thing.

ALVIN: Why?

ERROL: Well, didn't you eat much out there?

ALVIN: Yeah, course I ate.

ERROL: Well, you must have had some rice and goat. What about saltfish and johnny cakes?

ALVIN: Yeah, I see now. Yeah.

ERROL: You know what she's cooked you?

ALVIN: Lemme guess. Could it be…or no, it couldn't be.

ERROL: Go on. Have a shot in the dark.

ALVIN: Er, er…

ERROL: Yes Mr Marshall, Mr Alvin Marshall. For one thousand pounds can you tell me the recipe of the day?

ALVIN: Well, I'm not sure about it but… You've really got me there, Hughie.

ERROL: Oh come now, your time's running out. Five…four… three…two…one…

ALVIN: I've got it! Is it…is it flat meat and two veg?

ERROL: Correct! And here is your delicious first prize in place of the cash advertised. *(He comes through with the food.)* One sumptuous plate of flat meat and two veg with the added delight of one or two potatoes liberally sprinkled around. But hold it a minute. Hold it! Could they possibly be yam in disguise? He goes in a little closer to inspect the evidence only to find that, much to the crowd's astonishment… *(ALVIN catches his breath.)* …they're potatoes.

(ALVIN lets his breath out.)

73

ALVIN: Cheers.

ERROL: My pleasure.

ALVIN: If you look at the top of that bag… *(Pointing with his knife.)* I've brought summat back for you both, though it ain't much.

ERROL: Raas man! Me best go check it out, nuh.

(He gets up.)

ALVIN: If you want.

ERROL: Raas!

ALVIN: Hey! Don't rip the fucking bag apart.

ERROL: Well, where is it then?

ALVIN: I said, it's at the top.

ERROL: Is it fuck.

ALVIN: It is.

ERROL: Is this hide and seek or something?

ALVIN: Jesus! Look, I'll get it. You're as subtle as a fucking customs officer.

(He moves to get up.)

ERROL: No, I've got it. Is this it?

ALVIN: Yeah. They're both in it.

ERROL: Well one of 'em's a bottle. Is that for me?

ALVIN: Is it fuck.

ERROL: What is it?

ALVIN: Take it out and see.

ERROL: Rum!

ALVIN: Well, she likes it, don't she?

ERROL: A bit, I suppose.

ALVIN: Well, it'll last. It was all I could get through customs. I was gonna try and bring her back some of the white rum in a pop bottle, but I knew they'd rumble that one straight away.

ERROL: If it's the same shit as she got sent over at Christmas, fucking glass'll have melted before you got to England. *(Holds up a wooden Afro comb.)* Is this mine?

ALVIN: Yeah.

ERROL: *(Trying it out.)* It's alright.

ALVIN: It looks like your hair ain't seen a comb in weeks.

ERROL: Just got up, ain't I. It's great. Where'd you get it?

ALVIN: It's African. Check the carving. Done in Yoruba.

ERROL: Where's that?

ALVIN: Africa. I said it's African.

ERROL: Me ain't stupid, you know. Where in Africa, man?

ALVIN: Nigeria.

ERROL: Cool. Them is cool. Craftsmen.

ALVIN: Is this all she cooked?

ERROL: Yeah.

ALVIN: Fuck me. She must think I'm on a diet or something.

ERROL: She's been feeding us for years as if we were both on a fucking diet, or have you just noticed? *(Pause.)* Hey, hang on a minute.

75

ALVIN: I ain't off nowhere.

ERROL: How come it says 'Made in Hong Kong' on here. You lying bastard.

ALVIN: Oh come off it, man. I told you it's Yoruban. African.

ERROL: Africa fucking Hong Kong, you tight bastard.

ALVIN: No, you're wrong. Let me have a look.

(ALVIN comes across to him.)

ERROL: Here.

ALVIN: I don't see anything. Where's it say Hong Kong?

ERROL: On the other side, jewboy.

ALVIN: Oh dear. Yes, Errol, you're right. Take it back straight away.

ERROL: You cunt, you stuck it on didn't you?

ALVIN: Me? Oh no, not me. Trades Description Act, old boy. I wouldn't be so deceitful. I'll finish this and then take it back to the shop I bought it from.

ERROL: Give us it back, bastard.

ALVIN: That's gratitude for you.

(He gets up and takes his plate through to the kitchen.)

ERROL: Hey, England are getting some more black players in the squad.

ALVIN: About time. How's West Brom doing?

ERROL: Okay, I suppose. They're signing up some new brothers too.

ALVIN: No.

ERROL: What do you mean, no?

ALVIN: Well, what I meant was how are they doing in the league, you know? Results, since I've been away.

ERROL: Not too good. Lost 3-0 to Leeds last week and 4-2 at Palace on Saturday.

ALVIN: *(Comes back through.)* Brilliant!

ERROL: What you on about?

ALVIN: Well, you claim to support this team.

ERROL: So what? Anyhow, how come you ain't talking black?

ALVIN: What?

ERROL: You know. You've been over there for a while now and I thought you might have picked up a bit of the lingo. You know, add a bit of authenticity to the banter.

ALVIN: Oh that lingo. The English language.

ERROL: Shut up, prick! You know what I mean. You ain't come up with a single new 'un yet.

ALVIN: I tell you what I did see though.

ERROL: What?

ALVIN: A rasta football team.

ERROL: Bollocks.

ALVIN: No, I'm tellin' you. The Dreadlocks. AFC Dreadlocks. You know, like AFC Bournemouth. They play in red, green and gold stripes.

ERROL: Are you serious?

ALVIN: When they go up for a header, man, they go up high. Talk about floating about at the far post waiting for a cross.

ERROL: You're bullshitting.

ALVIN: I've got pictures, man. *(Gets up.)* Here, I'll get 'em.
They aren't very good 'cos it's that instant Polaroid thing
that Vernice lent us but you'll see. *(Sits.)* There.

ERROL: Bloody hell! I thought you were bulling me up!
Do they have any crowd trouble?

ALVIN: Are you kidding? By half-time most of the crowd are
asleep, man. By full time they're on a different planet.
It could be fucking ice hockey as far as they knew.

ERROL: God, and that's the harbour, isn't it?

ALVIN: Yeah.

ERROL: What's that?

ALVIN: That's the house we lived in, don't you remember?

ERROL: Yeah, course. Just vaguely.

ALVIN: Bollocks! You were only two when we left.

ERROL: Well, you were hardly a fucking pensioner at five.

ALVIN: But I remember more than you.

ERROL: Did they all remember you?

ALVIN: Most of them.

ERROR: Have you got a picture of me dad's cricket gear
on display?

ALVIN: No.

ERROL: Why not?

ALVIN: It wasn't there.

ERROL: Oh yeah? Someone must know. She said it was on
display in some sort of cabinet in the Civic Hall, what

78

with him being the first from the island to get selected for the full team.

ALVIN: Yeah I know, but it wasn't there.

ERROL: Someone must have known where it was, didn't you ask?

ALVIN: Course I asked and...

ERROL: And?

ALVIN: And nothing. Our Uncle, her brother, said he thought all that gear had been buried with him, then he pissed off without saying another word. Looked at me like I was mad, or something. *(Pause.)* She was probably just bragging, bullshitting us.

ERROL: She gets on my fucking tits sometimes.

ALVIN: Oh come on, man.

ERROL: 'Oh come on, man,' nothing. You know where she is, don't you?

ALVIN: I had put two and two together, but what d'you expect?

ERROL: You what? You don't know what it's been like living with the big white chief for the last two fucking weeks. You know what she called us all?

ALVIN: Who all?

ERROL: The Black Front.

ALVIN: What?

ERROL: Drug addicts and jigaboos. She's off her fucking head. How do you think I'm gonna feel going down Ram Jams and having to face that lot and tell them that I couldn't even persuade me own mother to join the strike?

ALVIN: They'll understand.

ERROL: Understand what? It's okay for you 'cos you've been off the frontline for a couple of weeks. It's me that's gonna get all the blame.

ALVIN: Everyone knows she's different.

ERROL: Everyone knows she's weak.

ALVIN: Look, it's over with, man. Cool it, okay? Just cool it. We can't do anything about it. It's her y'ought to let burn herself out, not you. It's her problem, right? It happened and it ain't worth arguing about.

ERROL: Okay then. What about the fucking milkman? He's working too.

ALVIN: Who, Stanley?

ERROL: The same. Vernice has just been round talking shit about how he'll lose his whole business if he strikes, and how everyone knows he's essential anyway so what's the point.

ALVIN: And?

ERROL: Essential my arse. If they all want a pint of milk they can go and buy it and all the black people in the area should have the sense already to buy in enough milk for the next two days.

ALVIN: Look, he's got a point.

ERROL: Like fuck.

ALVIN: I'm not sure about the strike myself anymore.

ERROL: Bollocks! You turned white en route, or what?

ALVIN: Look at it logically.

ERROL: Which is how I think I do but go on.

ALVIN: We all strike for two days, right?

ERROL: Right.

ALVIN: Buy nothing British, don't go to work, stay off the transport. In other words, stay out of sight, apart from those walking to see friends or relatives.

ERROL: Right.

ALVIN: Well, think of this then, and just imagine it. Two old men sat on a park bench an hour ago, or in two hours' time or any time tomorrow. One says to the other: 'Just like the old days, eh? Glad to be rid of the black bastards.' Other one agrees: 'Aye, pity we can't have this permanent. You know, all the time. No blacks in sight.' They think for a while and then one says to the other: 'I suppose we could, couldn't we?' 'Yeah, we could,' he says back. 'Where do you find the number of the National Front? Oh, I know. Let's look it up in the white pages.' The pair of them get up and go off to fucking do something about it.

ERROL: Very funny. Great story. You should be on telly. Basically, you're jacking out aren't you? You're fucking scared now.

ALVIN: These two old men, what they don't know is, fuck, isn't it inconvenient that the buses and the tubes and the trains are running a reduced service. What they don't think is, fuck, without the black doctors and nurses in this country the hospitals face crisis. What they don't think is, fuck, a few factories have got to shut down production for a while and the paki-shop isn't open. These aren't problems to worry about anymore; they're a challenge. They can, and will, be solved as quickly as possible, even if it means bringing in the fucking army. Stanley might just have a point.

ERROL: And you think she might too?

81

ALVIN: I don't know. Maybe. It's just not that simple, man.

ERROL: Jesus!

(Long pause.)

ALVIN: Have you been out today?

ERROL: I told you, I've only just got up.

ALVIN: Well, look, man, you're going to find out anyway. The streets are full of black people doing shopping, buying clothes, newspapers, getting taxis and so on. It's not working, man. It was never gonna really work.

ERROL: So whose side are you on now, then?

ALVIN: Whose side?

ERROL: You fucking heard!

ALVIN: Mine.

ERROL: And what about the plan; are you frightened of that too? Well? I've spent four weeks casing that joint and we ain't gonna get caught if that's what's worrying you. The plans are right here. Here *(He pulls out the box and begins to arrange the contents on the floor.)* Four weeks it's taken me to do all this, right down to how long the traffic lights stay on red at every junction within half a mile of the bank. It's practically fucking foolproof and you're jacking!

ALVIN: Who says I am? I never said anything about the job. I was talking about the strike and why that's jacked itself.

ERROL: You mean you still wanna do the job?

ALVIN: Yeah.

ERROL: Yeah? Just like we planned?

ALVIN: Yeah.

82

ERROL: I've got the armour upstairs, you know. Two rifles, two pistols like we said. You can't jack now.

ALVIN: I said yeah. I ain't jacking.

ERROL: Thank God for that. I thought you'd turned fucking yellow.

ALVIN: Me?

ERROL: Yes man, you. Boy, you take a lot off me mind. Gimme one drink, nuh. Drinka water.

ALVIN: Okay, cool it, that's all. Just cool it.

(ALVIN goes for a glass of water.)

ERROL: Yeah, okay, man. Okay, but you had me shitless. *(Pause.)* I still think you're full of shit about the strike though. Probably just bad leadership if it's not fully operational, but I guess it'll be alright as long as you don't break it.

(ALVIN comes in and gives him the water.)

ALVIN: Why shouldn't I break it?

ERROL: For fuck's sake, man.

ALVIN: It'll be perfect cover.

ERROL: Come on, man. Everyone from here to the fucking CIA probably knows you're a member of the Black Front.

ALVIN: Reformed member. No threat, no surveillance.

ERROL: Look, what is this shit, man? I thought you were tired?

ALVIN: I am.

ERROL: Well, why the fuck are you pissing me up with all these games, then?

ALVIN: I told you, man. We'll do the job just as I've planned it.

ERROL: Okay, man. I'm sorry.

ALVIN: There'll be one small difference, though.

ERROL: What small difference?

ALVIN: The money.

ERROL: What about the fucking money? I told you we'll take about five thousand minimum.

ALVIN: I want to keep back five hundred.

ERROL: No man, the Black Front needs it all. What do you want go thief five hundred for.

ALVIN: You haven't let me finish.

ERROL: Listen, man. If we donate a sum that size we're soon gonna be running the Black Front anyway, then we can do what we like with the money. Take back a thousand or two thousand or even everything, but why risk the leadership for five hundred! The papers are bound to print how much we take so they'll know we ripped them off.

ALVIN: I want you to take the five hundred and go for a holiday in the Caribbean.

ERROL: Bollocks, you ain't serious. I ain't fucking Ronald Biggs, you know. I stay here and use the money with the Black Front.

ALVIN: It's the only reason I'm doing the job, man. I want you to go home for yourself and see it so I don't have to explain to you why I think different now. I want you to see it with your own eyes, man.

ERROL: Look, if that's all it is I can get hold of a different five hundred tomorrow and piss off, but the job, man. You must do the job for the Black Front and nothing else or it's not right, man.

ALVIN: Where's this five hundred coming from?

ERROL: A friend. No bollocks. I can get it.

ALVIN: Sure?

ERROL: Sure I'm sure.

ALVIN: I mean, can you get it tomorrow? I mean just lay your hands on it?

ERROL: I can get it any time, man.

ALVIN: Right, that's settled then.

ERROL: What's settled?

ALVIN: I'm not doing the job.

ERROL: What the fuck's got into you? You find God over there or something?

ALVIN: You know how we always used to talk about 'truth' and the 'fight'?

ERROL: You mean in those long dim days of the week before last?

ALVIN: Well, what is it man, that West Indians here always mention when they talk about home?

ERROL: Come on, man.

ALVIN: I'll tell you. The weather. The weather, Errol, and picking fucking mangos off a tree. They've been here too long. You know what it's really like, man, and the same will be true in Africa. It's full of all the diseases of decolonisation, which they don't realise has eaten away at

85

their islands in the sun. Inflation, unemployment, political violence – remember them? Fucking weather! And then when I tried to talk to them, our own relatives, not just any black people, you know how they treated me? Like a stranger in a very strange land, and that's how I felt. Alone, man. And they don't see it like we do over here.

ERROL: I'm not surprised they ignored you. Seems like you turned into a white man as you crossed the International Date Line or something. A curious phenomenon of the native son looking down his nose at his own fucking people.

ALVIN: You think I did that? You of all fucking people.

ERROL: Course you did, or why else would they cut you dead? It's too late for me to become a part of the white world, but I notice you're still trying like fuck.

ALVIN: Look man, you'd better decide how much of you is Biko and how much is BSc. Econ. before the shit hits the fan because when it does you're going to have to run somewhere for cover, and if your own family won't give it to you, and there's no refuge in your place of birth, then where the fuck are you gonna go? Well?

ERROL: And which white boy's gonna let you hide behind him? Hang on, I know, I've heard this shit before, on the telly. You're gonna fight for the dispossessed and oppressed of the world, regardless of colour, starting right here in Britain on your own doorstep. Isn't that it? 'Dispossessed and oppressed versus the rest'. Well fuck me!

ALVIN: I'm going to train as…

ERROL: It's just so fucking predictable. A social worker! Three cheers for the community-minded negro.

ALVIN: Look, what the hell were we fighting for?

ERROL: What were we fighting for?

ALVIN: A place in the sun? In Montego Bay or Nairobi perhaps. It's fucking pointless when you've got enough fucking problems sitting on a beach in Brighton without getting your head kicked in by a bunch of bastard Hell's Angels.

ERROL: Well, you fucking explain to them that you're a social worker and not a black man as they get out their crowbars and jacks to mash up your fucking head with.

ALVIN: I'll explain, but I'll stay here and do it, not take up my arse somewhere else and talk shit up to my arse in genuine authentic black poverty.

ERROL: Look Al, man. Is this some kind of stunt you've been thinking up on the plane? Well, come on man. If it is it's worked, okay. Good job. Congratulations and all that. Well? I'm convinced. You fooled me. Hey!

ALVIN: A lot can happen in two weeks.

ERROL: Bollocks, man. Come on, man. Hey!

ALVIN: Errol, I went a third of the way round the world and back. I didn't just go to college for a term, or up to Leicester on an anti-Nazi rally. This was like an explosion in my head, man. It was as if I was seeing all the scaffolding I had built my life on suddenly collapsing, and out of this rubble I had to quickly build up something new otherwise I was finished. I'm not joking. I couldn't talk to them, man. They kept looking at me as if they felt sorry for me, as if I was a victim or something, so what the fuck could I do, man, except drive myself sick with question after question – asking myself stupid fucking questions.

ERROL: So you've decided we're better off here?

ALVIN: Yes, man.

ERROL: We're better off forgetting the strike and the job, we'd best forget we're black – turn the other cheek – settle down and get a fucking job, just sit back and wait, just hang out happy niggers playing ball or talking integration till it happens.

ALVIN: Till what happens?

ERROL: Fucking genocide. Being black isn't a gimmick, you know.

ALVIN: To you it's more a gimmick than you realise. West Brom and black players in the English squad, black talk this, and Africa that, baldhead and arming the community. Jesus, Errol, we've forgotten a lot between us.

ERROL: Forgotten what? You might have forgotten.

ALVIN: Unity, man.

ERROL: How the fuck can I unite with you, uncle? You're the one who's done the forgetting. You've forgotten what it's like to be stopped in the street and searched for no reason. You've forgotten what it's like to be called a nigger by a kid who's barely old enough to talk. You've forgotten what it's like to be beaten up at a football match, and as you lay in the St John's bit hear them all screaming in delight because someone's scored. It's only later that you discover it's the new black centre-forward who's scored. He's not a 'fucking nigger'. Well, not till he gets changed anyway. And you've forgotten why I wear a nine-inch scar on my leg.

ALVIN: Of course I haven't.

ERROL: 'Against the wall motherfucker! What was that boy? I hate you niggers…'

ALVIN: Look man I was there and…

ERROL: 'I'm gonna cut your balls off if I hear another word...'

ALVIN: Errol, for Christ's sake!

ERROL: 'An active buck, eh? Give me his knife, Constable. Wouldn't it be ironic if I used his own knife to cut off his balls. Keep still, nigger, or I'll cut you for real, boy! You black bastard...! Aghhh!'

ALVIN: You sick bastard, shut up! For God's sake shut up!

ERROL: Shut up! Shut up! Shut up! What the fuck do you know now, but shut up! All this crap about your life collapsing and you rebuilding it. You rebuilt nothing bastard, you just collapsed. You bastard!

ALVIN: That's right, I'm a bastard. Vera let that one slip, I've got to question it, man... I've got to find new order...

ERROL: Oh big fucking deal out there. That's a plus for me fucking mother as far as I'm concerned. Fucking white man's morals!

ALVIN: But...

ERROL: But you know nothing! You're finished! You're no more stable than a bleeding spinning top on its last rotation. What about me dad's gear?

ALVIN: I don't know. I told you.

ERROL: What about me dad's grave? I noticed there weren't a picture of that either, even though I asked you for one specially. Didn't they tell you where it was? Well, social worker? Well!

ALVIN: It's unmarked, they said.

ERROL: Unmarked! Filled you with some shit, didn't they? Star fucking West Indian cricketer in unmarked grave! I'll bet me dad's pissing himself at your initiative. Bloody disgrace you are! Brush you off with any old shit! Probably felt sorry for you, all intense and committed. Couldn't even talk to his own people on their level. Me dad would puke if he could see you!

ALVIN: And what the fuck right have you got to talk about him?

ERROL: As much right as you'll ever have. He'd have done something about it.

ALVIN: About what?

ERROL: About everything! He wouldn't have turned into some baldhead, weak-kneed, pink-arse, talking down to his own black people and crying for sympathy when he can't get no fucking answers.

ALVIN: You don't know.

ERROL: Oh, I fucking know alright 'cos he's my dad too, not just yours. *(Picks up a picture of his mother off the top of the cabinet and smashes it down.)* This is all you're fucking worth now, white boy.

ALVIN: Stop it!

ERROL: Why don't you get your pink-arse out to work and join her or go phone the bank and warn them that you know of a black nigger who's bad and gonna pull a job? My dad would have kicked your fuckin' head in! He'd have swept aside all this shit and got to the heart of the matter. Fear! You're shit-scared now!

(He sweeps all the pictures off the cabinet top, pulls the mirror down off the wall, and begins to stamp on it.)

ALVIN: You mad bastard, stop it! Stop it!

(They fight. Eventually ERROL knocks ALVIN out. He hits his head as he falls. ERROL picks up his box and things and slowly makes

90

*his way out. He is bruised and dazed. As he shuts the door ALVIN
begins to stir. He is going to be alright.)*

(The lights come down.)

END OF ACT TWO

Act Three

SCENE ONE

Lights up. Tuesday evening. We see ALVIN lying on the settee, holding a pack of ice to his eye which is blackened. The damaged pictures are back on top of the cabinet, and the mirror lies discarded in one corner. He is thinking uncomfortable thoughts.

We hear the door open and slam. MOTHER enters. At first she doesn't notice ALVIN then she sees his feet.

MOTHER: Alvin? *(She moves around.)* Alvin, what's happened? What's the matter with you?

ALVIN: Nothing, I'm alright.

MOTHER: What's the matter? What happened? Don't tell me nothing. I'm not blind.

ALVIN: I had an argument with Errol.

MOTHER: An argument?

ALVIN: A fight.

MOTHER: About what?

ALVIN: Nothing. I asked for it, I suppose. I'll be alright. It's just a bruise.

MOTHER: What the hell were you fighting over?

ALVIN: Nothing, I said. Let's just forget it.

MOTHER: I can't just forget it like that. Where is he?

ALVIN: I don't know. Down the club, I suppose. I didn't ask.

(MOTHER puts down her bag and takes off her coat.)

MOTHER: *(Unwinding a little.)* When did you get back?

92

ALVIN: A couple of hours ago.

MOTHER: That was quick.

ALVIN: What was?

MOTHER: The flight.

ALVIN: The flight was on time. I got a lift from the airport.

MOTHER: Who from?

ALVIN: Just someone I met on the plane, that's all. *(Sits up.)* Why, didn't you want to see me?

MOTHER: Don't be silly. Of course I want to see you, it's just that I thought I'd be back before you got here. I left something for you in the oven in case I wasn't. Did you get it?

ALVIN: Yeah, Errol gave it to me. *(Gets up.)* Do you want a cup of coffee or something?

MOTHER: I'll get it.

(She goes through into the kitchen and he sits down again.)

How was home, then? *(No answer.)* Well, how was it?

ALVIN: The worst two weeks of my life.

(Long pause. MOTHER comes back through with her drink.)

MOTHER: Errol was…

ALVIN: I don't want to talk about Errol. I've said all I've got to say to him.

MOTHER: Well, I thought he'd be glad to have you back. I'm glad to have you back. Can I give you a hug? I suppose you think you're too old to kiss your mother now… *(She hugs him but gets no response.)*

What's the matter? Is there something you want to tell me?

ALVIN: Was it a joke?

MOTHER: Was what a joke?

ALVIN: Sending me out there?

MOTHER: But you said you wanted to go.

ALVIN: Did I?

MOTHER: Alvin, when the telegram came...

ALVIN: When the telegram came you looked at it for an hour then opened it and told us that your dad was dead. Told us our grandfather, who neither of us can remember anyway, was dead. Then you went to get a cup of coffee, mumbling something about time off work being hard to get, and by the time you came back through with the three cups of coffee you'd had an idea. Why didn't I represent the three of us at the funeral? Give me a chance to see the island. Course I wanted to go!

MOTHER: But...

ALVIN: But under the circumstances, mother, I think you should have done your own dirty work.

MOTHER: What happened?

ALVIN: Oh, so you were expecting something to happen?

MOTHER: No I just want to know what all this is about. I sent you out there to my father's funeral because...

ALVIN: Yes, we know. Because you couldn't afford time off from work. I suppose all my life I've wanted to go back. All I really remembered about the island was leaving it and getting on a big dirty boat, full of scruffy, dirty people, as a confused kid of five. All that pushing and shouting. Historically I suppose it was a kind of second diaspora but all I knew was that my world was turning upside down and I clung tightly to your hand not knowing what the hell was going on. *(Pause.)* You know, for the last nineteen years I've wondered about that island, mother, about the people on it, what they're doing, who they are, and why I'm not back there with them, sitting in the sun and living the simple life of existence, with no worries and all that. I've wondered what I'd have been like if I'd stayed there, what I'd have done, and then it kept dawning on me that l shouldn't really be wondering at all. You should be telling me. You know, filling in the blanks 'cos the most important part of knowing where you're going to is knowing where you've come from, right? *(Pause.)* I guess till I was eighteen and went to university it was pretty easy. I worried but it was a kind of part-time worry 'cos my schoolwork was something I could channel all that energy and panic into. Try and prove something, I guess. An island unto myself and all that. But all that changed at university, especially in the last year where you've suddenly got to face the sick reality that your life's about to take a turn which'll nine times out of ten put you on the road you'll have to follow forever. Now what was I, a black boy who came from an island three thousand miles away, doing in the posh white university? Mother, what the hell did that dirty, scruffy, stinking boat have to do with all that lecturing and books, all that wealth and bloody ceremony? You've never talked to us. None of you do. To leave that place and get a 'proper job' or start a bloody career wasn't gonna give us any answers, it wasn't gonna give me any answers, it would probably just negate any chance of me ever finding them, so I decided to drop out, to hover in mid-air, and for the last two and a half years I've just waited and waited. Plenty of hollow rhetoric, plenty of passionate intensity, but still no answers. And then my grandfather died and you suggested I went 'home' and I thought yes, 'home', and yes, this is Babylon and yes, yes, yes I've got to go to my

95

people and yes, I should have just got a job, any job, and saved and gone a long time ago, and yes, when I get back I want to take off for Africa so yes, I'll have to make plans to have some bread available to depart soon after I get back and we take over the leadership and yes, Errol was coming too. Answers. At last it was all happening, mother. The oscillation and the vacancy seemed to be coming to an end. First the West Indies then plunge into the deep end and visit the mother country – Africa. I bought a notebook in which I was going to keep notes for a book I was going to write about my two weeks in the West Indies and my trip to Africa. *Out of Exile: Free at Last* by Alvin Marshall. My first bestseller. Well go on then, laugh.

MOTHER: I'm not laughing, Alvin. Go on. What happened, please?

ALVIN: 'What happened, please!'

MOTHER: Alvin.

ALVIN: You know what they call you, mother? That is if they can be bothered to think of you in the first place. 'Miss Chalkie'. That's about as big an insult as they can think of. They daren't call you anything obscene, not that they don't want to, in case someone finds it funny. That's a measure of their hatred for you. They don't even laugh about you. After all this time you're not even a joke. I don't know why they bothered to send you the telegram. They knew you wouldn't come. I think they just wanted to make you feel guilty.

MOTHER: Alvin, listen to me…

ALVIN: No! You listen to me. Let me say what I've got to say, please. Your sister, Vera, met me at the airport. She was about the only one who talked to me the whole time I was there. She took me back to the house where I met your mother and brother too. It was getting late so the four of us sat down for a meal and we were getting on fine, or so I thought, until I told them how sorry you were that you hadn't been able to make it for the funeral. 'Oh,' said Vera. Your mother started to cry so your brother took her into the other room. They didn't come out till I'd gone to bed. The next day I went for a walk with Vera and she asked after you and Errol, and Vernice and Charmain. So I told her how things were and how they were in England and what we were trying to do. She didn't give a damn really, so I spent the next few days on my own, taking pictures, talking to nobody, buying my own food in cafes, and just coming back there to sleep. It was obvious they didn't really want me there. Then the day of the funeral came. I didn't have a suit so your brother lent me one and I went. When we came back he asked for his suit, told me to get out, and to tell you not to bother ever coming back. It was as simple as that. I'd come for the funeral, it was over now so I had to go. Oh, I nearly forgot. He told me to tell you that your mother never wants to see you again. I tried to tell him I had two more days before the plane I was booked on left, but he just laughed. So I spent the last two days in a rooming house with no money spare to buy food. Time to do plenty of thinking and writing in, I thought. Well, I certainly did a lot of thinking, but here... *(He gets up and goes across to his bags.)* ...let me show you the notes I made for my first bestseller; that first classic of decolonisation. See, nothing. Absolutely nothing. Not only had my family treated me like a leper, but the island itself was just riddled with corruption. Smuggling at customs was so open and institutionalised, I couldn't believe it. I was too ashamed of my own people to write down what I found. *(Pause.)* Well, haven't you got anything to say, mother? You know full well what you were sending me out there for, so why didn't you tell me you were persona non grata; that we all are. You know what they think of us? They think we're cowards. White cowards.

97

MOTHER: Let them think what they want.

ALVIN: Do what, mother? You'll have to do a little better than that this time.

MOTHER: Listen to me, son.

ALVIN: Mother, I was born out of wedlock, right? Well? Okay, I'm a bastard. Where's my father's grave? Where's his cricket gear on display? I sat in that rooming house for two days, frightened sick to go to the Town Hall and look up the answers in the records there. I was frightened of what I might find. Well? Okay then, don't look so surprised.

MOTHER: I meant to tell you.

ALVIN: Like hell!

MOTHER: I wanted to tell you but I thought it might upset you.

ALVIN: Upset me?

MOTHER: I don't want to hurt any of you with this kind of thing. It's not important is it?

ALVIN: I wouldn't have cared less about being told I was a bastard, that's how much it would have upset me!

MOTHER: But I wasn't to know that.

ALVIN: Where's my father's grave? Where's this display of his cricket gear?

MOTHER: Didn't anyone tell you?

ALVIN: Why the hell should anyone tell me? Why the hell should I have to ask? Where! Where! Where!

MOTHER: I don't know.

ALVIN: What's that supposed to mean?

MOTHER: I mean, Alvin, that I've never seen your father's grave. He didn't die of cancer before we left. *(Pause.)* He was alive. He died only about two years ago. Vera wrote and told me about it.

ALVIN: You mean he's been alive all these years you've been telling us he was dead, and you knew about it?

MOTHER: You've got to understand, Alvin, that I couldn't tell you about it.

ALVIN: What do you mean you couldn't? You mean you wouldn't. You...you...

MOTHER: He was no good for you all. That's why we left him behind and escaped to England.

ALVIN: What do you mean, escaped? What was he, a mass fucking murderer or something?

MOTHER: Your father was a cricketer, like I've always told you, but he took to drink and I didn't want my children brought up in a house with a drunk. Sometimes he'd disappear for days, and then come in in the middle of the night and smash up the furniture in his drunken rage. He'd wake you all up with the noise, take whatever money I had, and that would be the last we'd see of him for a few more days. What the hell did you want me to do? Let it go on until one day he turned on one of us and killed us? It was a living hell, Alvin. I couldn't cope with you all and him and anyhow, what kind of an education did you think you were all going to get on that island? What kind of life were we going to be able to lead with him acting like an animal? What kind of life was I going to have?

ALVIN: What did you do to him?

MOTHER: What did I do to him?

ALVIN: What did you do to him? Cricketers don't just suddenly go mad overnight for no reason. Gary Sobers didn't go out and knock up two hundred one day, and come out to bowl in a straitjacket and foaming at the mouth the next. *(Pause.)* Or was he mad when you eventually decided to make it legal?

MOTHER: Alvin!

ALVIN: Well, come on. Was he mad when you married him, or did you drive him round the bloody bend?

MOTHER: No.

ALVIN: Well, what did you do to him, then? What did you do to drive my father mad and leave him to an unmarked grave?

MOTHER: Nothing. It was him.

ALVIN: Well, I'm waiting.

MOTHER: When he was picked for the team for the second time.

ALVIN: The West Indies?

MOTHER: Yes.

ALVIN: Well?

MOTHER: Well, he tried to organise a boycott and come out on strike. He wanted the team to refuse to play.

ALVIN: Why?

MOTHER: Because, Alvin, you've got to understand that up until then the captain of the West Indies had always been white and your father felt it ought to be a black man. He wanted to be captain himself, and everyone said he ought to be the captain. He was, Alvin, the best all-rounder the island had ever seen. Wallace Marshall. He could do it all, son.

ALVIN: And what happened?

MOTHER: Nobody signed their contracts and it looked
like the tour was off unless Wallace was made captain
but... But, someone from London flew out and offered
everybody except Wallace twice the money, plus bonuses,
to sign up.

ALVIN: And?

MOTHER: And? They signed of course. Three days later the
team took off on the tour without your father.

ALVIN: Still with a white captain?

MOTHER: Your father's life collapsed, Alvin. He lived for
cricket. He knew nothing else, so what else could he do?
He started to drink. Errol was only a few months old at
the time, and at first I managed to hide it from my parents.
But then he came round one time in a drunken rage when
Vernice and Wilfred were visiting. They felt they ought to
get Wallace some help so they told my mother, who came
to live with us, and my father offered to look after Wallace.
He wouldn't have it. He said he wanted us, his family,
and my mother left. The day she left us and Wallace came
back was the last time I saw her, but it was no good.
I didn't want to live with a drunk, I didn't want you all
to...to... *(She begins to cry.)*

ALVIN: Mother...

MOTHER: No, I want to go on. You said you wanted to hear.
What the hell was I supposed to do, then? Hope you all
wouldn't notice, that it would all go away like magic? Well,
it wasn't going away, Alvin. It was getting worse. I had to
get out. We had to get out. So we came to England.

ALVIN: We ran away to England.

MOTHER: We had to, Alvin.

ALVIN: Why didn't you tell us all this before instead of just pretending.

MOTHER: I didn't want you to make him into an idol of some kind, a hero.

ALVIN: Well, what's all this about a display of his cricket gear, then? And what's all this about telling us how good he was... What's that if not making a hero out of him?

MOTHER: But I wanted you to be proud of him. You should be proud of him, but not follow him. You've both got an education and advantages that he never had and I've worked myself stupid to get you where you are now. You can stand up on your own two feet and rise up out of the gutter. I just don't understand why you all want to wallow in the filth and...

ALVIN: Is that what you think of Vernice, then? The gutter. Wallowing in filth with no education, no certificates.

MOTHER: No, of course not...

ALVIN: But we're better? My father probably died a tramp and a broken man. A drunk. Vernice's husband died an electrician. He died in his sleep in the warmth of his English bed. I can live with what my father was. I could have lived with it before, but don't you think Errol has a right to know about him now?

MOTHER: Errol has problems of his own.

ALVIN: And you're the cause of most of them.

MOTHER: Not this one.

ALVIN: What one?

MOTHER: Shelley's pregnant.

ALVIN: What?

MOTHER: I didn't go to school today. I hardly slept for a
    moment last night worrying. I went and met Shelley as
    she was going to collect the results of her pregnancy test.
    Errol's going to be a father.

ALVIN: And does Errol know?

MOTHER: He may do by now. Shelley's gone to meet him
    at the club.

ALVIN: Jesus Christ! Did he know she thought she was pregnant?

MOTHER: No. Shelley didn't want to tell him till she was sure.

ALVIN: I don't believe it.

MOTHER: She said he was always in the wrong mood.

ALVIN: And of course you weren't going to tell your own son
    that he was well on the way to becoming a father.

MOTHER: I only found out yesterday.

ALVIN: If you can't tell your own son that he may be about to
    become a father then something is very wrong. You know,
    I just don't believe it! I thought I had it all worked out
    and everything. You know what I was gonna do, mother?
    Social work. I thought, if I'm gonna stay here I might
    as well contribute. This place, Britain, is full of shit, but
    where else is there? But mother! I can't stay here with you.
    Every time you open your mouth another pillar tumbles.
    One of us has to go. It's as simple as that. Either you leave
    me alone or I... I don't know. Leave us both alone.

MOTHER: What do you mean, Alvin?

ALVIN: I'll tell you what I mean. Remember the 1968
    Olympics and the John Carlos, Tommie Smith, Black
    Power thing, the salute; and I said to you in joy, how all
    the black people were winning for once, and how I was
    over the moon about it...and you hit me. And when

I wanted to do a project on sugar 'cos I knew it came
from the West Indies and you told me real sugar grew in
England and you said I had to do it on sugar beet. Okay.
And when I told you the reason you're still on the bottom
scale of teaching even though you're the highest qualified
and longest serving you shouted at me and then wouldn't
talk to me for days. Now is it just this bastard country or
is it the two of you in partnership that are dragging us
under? Good God, I go half way round the world and
back thinking I'd made some sort of discovery and come
back to find the same damn lies, the same white lies, the
same black lies. The same shame; the same fear; the same
shallowness. You're no better than Errol. You're different
sides of the same coin, but you're worse if anything 'cos
you've got the whole truth to play with and you still
distort it. You haven't even got the decency to afford
either of us that luxury. Why? Why?

MOTHER: For you! For you all! You two are all I've got.
Everything I've ever done has been for the two of you,
Alvin. Please leave me alone now. Can't you see that I did
it all for you?

ALVIN: Leave you alone? You who presides up above,
determining our destinies, keeping the answers to yourself
yet asking all the questions.

MOTHER: Stop it! Stop it!

ALVIN: Do you want to see us two end up in unmarked
graves, eh? Do you want to see Errol with a bottle in one
hand, banging his head against a brick wall like our dad?
You spend all day helping someone else's child...

MOTHER: What do you want me to do? Let her walk the
streets? Her parents are putting her out and do you want
me to let her panic and suffer because of my son?

ALVIN: Your son! He's no more your son than bloody
    Winston Churchill's your son. There's no point of contact.
    Oh, I'm sure you want to help Shelley through. After
    all, you can see her problem. It's material! It's physical.
    It's going to be born soon, but when it's black, when it's
    in the mind, you just run. You run as you ran from our
    dad and your family, and for years you've been running
    away from us. Did you think that going down to Ram
    Jams was a passing phase like a pop group or platform
    soles? Do you think that we don't want to be happy and
    have some money and live like everyone else? Do you
    think it's all just a big joke, or can't any of you see any
    further than your precious white respectability and your
    bastard mortgages? You've blown it this time, haven't
    you? It's your game, your rules. Well? Can't you see we
    need protecting? There's enough black people in lunatic
    asylums as it is. *(He gets up to move away.)*

MOTHER: Where are you going?

ALVIN: That's it? That's it exactly! Instead of saying 'don't
    go'! It's here! The facts in my opinion are this and I
    think you ought to consider that. It's just 'where are
    you going?' – 'you're wasting your life' – 'get a proper
    job' – 'dress smartly' – 'do up your tie' – clichés for the
    white boy! Well? Well no! I demand more than being told
    that I'm not in the gutter and that I'm to dress properly.
    I want to know why I'm black. I want to know all that
    you know about being black. I want to know what
    blackness has meant to you – to your father, or your
    father's father's father. I want to know how to defend
    myself. I want to know how you've defended yourself,
    how my father coped, how we all have got this far, and
    sadly only you can give me the answers, but you refuse. I
    don't want no Africa or Caribbean anymore; I don't want
    to compromise. I want answers, 'cos I'm going under,
    and if I'm not going to get any answers then I need help

but the only people who can help me are either too busy playing white or too busy playing black, understand! Understand!

MOTHER: Alvin!

ALVIN: I don't need your lies anymore. Not now, not ever. I've told you, it's me or you.

MOTHER: What do you want, Alvin?

ALVIN: Right now I want some ice for my eye.

(He goes into the kitchen to get some silence. We hear the back door open and shut.)

VERNICE: Is she back yet?

ALVIN: Through there.

VERNICE: What happen?

ALVIN: Nothing.

(VERNICE comes through. ALVIN slides the door shut behind her.)

VERNICE: What happen to Alvin?

MOTHER: He hurt his eye fighting with Errol.

VERNICE: Lord, me thought the pair uh them come too ol' for that sorta thing. What happen?

MOTHER: For Christ's sake, I don't want to talk about it, Vernice.

VERNICE: Girl, me tired like hell too, so don't bite off me head, huh.

MOTHER: I'm sorry.

VERNICE: Well, I tell you, you shoulda tell the boy. You can't say me ain't warn you. At least me try. Anyway, Stanley ask me to marry him again. Vivien?

MOTHER: I'm listening.

VERNICE: But...

MOTHER: But what?

VERNICE: Charmain leaving.

MOTHER: Leaving what?

VERNICE: Leaving home, leaving me because she say she hate Stanley, because she say she goin' hate me if I marry him.

MOTHER: Well, I don't know what to say.

VERNICE: *(Quietly.)* At least she talking to me again.

MOTHER: What are you going to do?

VERNICE: What can I do? I thought you might talk to her and explain.

MOTHER: Explain what, Vernice?

VERNICE: Explain that Stanley is a fine man, or mebbe you ain't think so?

MOTHER: Of course I do.

VERNICE: Do you know what the last eight years have been like for me without Wilfred, girl? The first few years me down the club so every night an' me doing it so often I think uh starting to charge, but Charmain too small to know about that. And then when she start to come bigger I try an' settle down with a man. You remember Charlie? Then Rudy? No-good bastards. Only Stanley's been any good to me, given me money an' love. Remember love?

MOTHER: I remember love.

VERNICE: Can't you talk to her?

MOTHER: It's blood they want, Vernice, not talking to.

VERNICE: Vivien, listen to me, girl. Me can't remember the last time I say please to you or anybody else, but can't you help me out please?

MOTHER: Vernice.

VERNICE: Can't you ask Alvin, then. Can't he come an' talk to she.

MOTHER: Alvin?

VERNICE: Why not? Me ain't thinka nobody else she goin' listen to.

(ALVIN opens the door and comes through. He has discarded the ice pack.)

ALVIN: What? Well you called me.

(He picks up his jacket.)

MOTHER: I wasn't calling you.

VERNICE: It was me. I wonder if you could come across an' talk to Charmain. She say she upset an' want to leave home.

ALVIN: What's the matter with her, then? Well? Why's she so upset?

VERNICE: I don't know but…

ALVIN: Well, when you find out let me know. I'm off for a walk round the block to get some fresh air.

MOTHER: Alvin.

ALVIN: Don't worry. I said I'm just going for a walk. I'll be back. I'm not gonna throw myself under a bus or anything. *(He goes.)*

VERNICE: Girl, don't look so. He ain't goin' do nothing stupid.

MOTHER: How do you know?

VERNICE: I don't. Me jus' trying to help. If you want make
an enemy outa me now, well jus' go ahead an' do it for me
think that be what you want.

MOTHER: Vernice, that's not what I want, and you know it.
I just want my kids back, that's all. I just want for us both
to be happy again.

VERNICE: Happy! Like when the hell the last time we both
happy together? I mean the botha us really happy? Never
in England. No.

(MOTHER begins to cry.)

Jesus girl, pull you all self together. People ain't take no
notice uh tears anymore. They gone outa fashion an' there
ain't much we can do about it.

MOTHER: Sorry.

VERNICE: But nothing to be sorry about. As for meself, well,
I suppose me gotta make a choice.

MOTHER: No you haven't.

VERNICE: No choice?

MOTHER: No choice.

VERNICE: Sharp as ever.

MOTHER: Wish I was.

VERNICE: Did you go to work today?

MOTHER: No.

VERNICE: I'm glad.

(They hug each other.)

I'll go telephone him and tell him it's just two pints a day and no cream from now on.

MOTHER: Wait! There's somebody at the door. I don't want to be alone if it's Errol.

VERNICE: Why? You had a bust-up with him too?

(Enter ERROL and SHELLEY from the hall. SHELLEY is carrying a suitcase.)

SHELLEY: Hello, Miss.

VERNICE: Boy, I hope you ain't come back here to cause you all mother no more trouble, for she got enough on she plate as it is.

ERROL: I ain't come back here to cause nobody any trouble, and I ain't come back to listen to you or anybody else, so why don't you just get off my back. When I wanna be insulted ask somebody black to do it. *(He moves to go upstairs.)*

SHELLEY: Shall... Shall I wait here, Errol?

ERROL: Wait there. *(Without turning to look at her he goes upstairs.)*

MOTHER: You better go and ring Stanley. I'll be alright now.

VERNICE: Girl, me ain't want to leave you if you is still so.

MOTHER: There's nothing to worry about, Vernice. I'll call round to see the pair of you later.

VERNICE: Girl, things looking better already. *(To SHELLEY.)* Don't let him bully you so. Tell him where to get off, you hear me?

SHELLEY: *(Nervously.)* Yes.

(VERNICE goes via the kitchen.)

MOTHER: Well?

SHELLEY: I waited for him by the club, Miss and…

MOTHER: And?

SHELLEY: And eventually he came down. I think he's fallen out with Alvin.

MOTHER: Go on.

SHELLEY: He told me to get lost, Miss, and then I told him, 'cos I thought he was going to hit me, but I didn't tell him that you knew or anything. I just said that I was having his baby and he laughed. He wasn't angry with me or anything, Miss, he just laughed, and then he kissed me and said we were going away.

MOTHER: Going away where?

SHELLEY: Africa, I think. He said we were going to have a warrior.

MOTHER: Oh my God!

SHELLEY: He said this warrior would come back and haunt you and everybody else. He said we'd have to get ready, for the time was near, so he sent me home to pack and get me things while he waited at the club for us. Me mum and dad were out for once and so I got everything and he's upstairs getting his stuff now.

MOTHER: You're going now?

SHELLEY: Yes, Miss. Tonight. Somewhere in Africa. Errol's going to get a job as an economic adviser to the freedom fighters.

MOTHER: What freedom fighters, Shelley?

SHELLEY: The African freedom fighters.

MOTHER: Africa? Tonight. For Christ's sake, Shelley, grow up.

SHELLEY: Miss?

MOTHER: What do you want, Shelley? I mean what do you really want more than anything else?

SHELLEY: Miss, I've never had nothing. It's easy for you but I love Errol and I want to have our baby. I might never get a second chance. Me mum and dad hate each other and since me dad got laid off at the factory last year it's just got worse. All he does is just stay in bed then go down the betting shop or the boozer and the only excitement he gets is telling me what a slut I am and hitting me mum. And she can't leave him 'cos she hasn't got anywhere else to go, Miss. She's older than him and in five or six years she'll be on her pension. You wouldn't think she was my mum if you saw her. When I said I wanted to stay on at school they said they'd kick me out. I told you that, Miss. I've got to fend for meself now.

MOTHER: Safety of a family? Protection?

SHELLEY: Suppose so, Miss. He'll have to love his baby at least.

MOTHER: And you love him?

SHELLEY: Yes, Miss.

MOTHER: You love him enough to leave schoolwork and your family? You love him enough to believe that he'll give you what you want, Shelley? 'Top of the Pops' security.

SHELLEY: Yes, Miss. We're having a baby, Miss.

MOTHER: You're so young.

SHELLEY: Everybody says that, but I don't feel it. I can look after meself.

MOTHER: Can you? Can you look after yourself and Errol? Can you look after yourself and Errol and the baby, Shelley?

112

SHELLEY: I won't have to Miss, cos there'll be Errol.

MOTHER: But Shelley, you're so sure.

SHELLEY: I've got to be, Miss, or I couldn't do it. I'm old enough to think for meself now.

MOTHER: You do realise that if you all give up, my children stand no chance.

SHELLEY: Miss?

MOTHER: Nothing, Shelley. Look, the African freedom fighters.

SHELLEY: Yes, Miss.

MOTHER: How are you going to get to Africa, Shelley?

SHELLEY: Errol's taking care of that.

MOTHER: He is, is he?

SHELLEY: Yes, Miss.

MOTHER: *(Goes for her handbag.)* Take this key, Shelley, and I want you to use it if you have to. It's the key to the front door.

SHELLEY: But Miss, Errol's got one.

MOTHER: Errol mustn't know that you've got one as well. My house is your house now, and I want you to remember that. If you don't want to go back to your parents, if things go wrong, then you don't have to, understand? I want you to take it.

SHELLEY: *(Takes the key.)* Okay. I'll be fine, Miss, but thanks anyway.

MOTHER: Promise you won't lose it.

SHELLEY: I won't lose it, Miss. Thanks.

(We hear a shot go off upstairs. SHELLEY screams.)

MOTHER: Oh my God!

(She restrains SHELLEY.)

SHELLEY: Errol? Errol!

MOTHER: Oh my God, no!

SHELLEY: Let me go, Miss. Let me go!

MOTHER: No! I'll go. I'm going. Stay here.

SHELLEY: *(Clawing at MOTHER.)* But, Miss. Let me go!

MOTHER: Shelley, stop it. Get off, Shelley. Leave me alone!

SHELLEY: Errol! Errol!

(MOTHER tries to break free and get upstairs. The front door crashes open and ALVIN comes in.)

ALVIN: What's happened?

(He doesn't wait for an answer. He rushes upstairs.)

MOTHER: *(Stays put.)* Oh my God, Errol.

SHELLEY: *(In tears.)* Miss, I love him.

(VERNICE rushes in.)

VERNICE: What was that? What's goin' on? Vivien?

SHELLEY: Errol's shot himself.

VERNICE: Oh my God! Is Alvin up there?

(SHELLEY nods.)

Jesus Christ! Ain't nobody goin' phone for the ambulance
or the police or what?

(She goes across to the phone and begins to dial. ALVIN comes down.)

114

ALVIN: Leave it.

VERNICE: But…

ALVIN: I said leave it. We don't need it.

(SHELLEY screams and MOTHER looks like she's going to faint.)

VERNICE: *(Runs to MOTHER.)* God have mercy on his soul.

ALVIN: He's alright.

SHELLEY: *(Goes towards the steps.)* Errol!

ALVIN: *(Holds her back.)* I said he's alright. He's coming down.

SHELLEY: Errol!

(Enter ERROL, with a suitcase and the brown parcel, which clearly contains the weapons. SHELLEY moves towards him but he stops her with his gaze.)

Are you okay, Errol?

ERROL: Course I'm okay. Just look at you all. A real picture of fucking concern. Don't worry. *(He gestures to the parcel.)* I'm taking them with me.

VERNICE: Boy, you sick.

ERROL: I'm sick? Me? Just take a look at yourselves.

VERNICE: Don't talk to you all mother so. Leave it for you stinking friends and that she there beside you, but you leave you mother outa this, you hear me?

ERROL: She is carrying my child. My baby. Surprised? Didn't think I knew what I was doing? You all didn't think I could hold the pressure, but we're all dead men talking to dead men but futility is no theory. It's not reality or brutality. My child shall live. It's a sign.

VERNICE: What is a sign?

ERROL: A child; my child.

VERNICE: You'd better ask she about that.

ERROL: It's either mine or it's an immaculate conception! A leader is born in the promised land.

VERNICE: Me better phone a doctor.

ALVIN: No.

MOTHER: *(Weakly.)* Errol, listen to me.

ERROL: Listen to you, mother? What, again? Listen to you some more, mother?

MOTHER: I want to talk with you. We all do.

ERROL: Oh, do we all?

MOTHER: Alvin and I…

ERROL: Oh, come now. Let's leave Snow White out of this.

VERNICE: You want to look to you woman, boy.

ERROL: Don't 'boy' me, woman. I don't give a fuck about her and she knows it.

MOTHER: Please listen, Errol.

ERROL: Go tell it to the white man but don't come tainting my black ears.

VERNICE: You nasty-minded little bastard.

ERROL: I think you've got the wrong one there.

ALVIN: Get out, Errol.

ERROL: Talking to me, nigger?

ALVIN: I said just go, for God's sake.

ERROL: You want me to black up your other eye, white boy?

ALVIN: For Christ's sake if you're going, then go, but leave her alone now.

ERROL: What, so you can comfort your mummy, Social Worker?

ALVIN: I've got no more comfort for her than I have for you, so just go.

ERROL: Don't you want to know where I'm going?

ALVIN: No.

ERROL: *(Pulls out five hundred pounds.)* Shelley's been peddling her arse. Doing a bit of whoring on the side for me.

SHELLEY: That's not true!

ALVIN: You bastard!

ERROL: *(Pulls out a knife.)* Another step, nigger, and I'll cut you so bad boy.

MOTHER: Shelley.

SHELLEY: It's my money, Miss, but I didn't.

VERNICE: You didn't what? Get your arse out of the house an' take him with you.

(ERROL picks up his suitcase and moves out towards the door.)

ERROL: I'm off to Africa. You're the ones that need a fucking doctor, not me.

(He goes towards the front door. SHELLEY picks up her case and follows him. She has no choice.)

VERNICE: The boy's sick.

MOTHER: Alvin, can't you stop him?

ALVIN: Stop him? Me stop him and you didn't even open your own mouth to stop him. He's gone out of that door as ignorant as he came in, and even after you've told me what you have, I'm still as ignorant as I was before. I don't understand what you're playing at. Stop him? I'm in no position to stop me, let alone him. Words can't stop him now. Words can't help.

VERNICE: You both want you all damn heads examining.

ALVIN: Listen, you better put your own house in order. You aren't exactly a paragon of virtue yourself.

VERNICE: I have done put me house in order an' I won't be makin' the same mistake again.

ALVIN: Well, think yourself lucky that you got to it before the dam broke 'cos some of us ain't so fucking fortunate.

(He storms upstairs.)

VERNICE: Are you alright, Vivien?

MOTHER: Alright? Alright! When my son's just left home after calling me everything under the sun. Every dirty, filthy name he could think of. Am I alright?

VERNICE: I sorry, girl. Why you not come and sit down, nuh? *(They go across and sit.)* What the boy doing with guns, anyhow?

MOTHER: Vernice, how the hell am I supposed to know! I'm just their mother, for God's sake! I just work my damn fingers to the bone for twenty-five and odd years, doing everything from typist to teacher so they have two crusts of bread on their plate and clothes on their backs. I just take them to a country halfway round the world, where they can live and grow up, I just turn my back on my own family for them, I just love once, just once, for them. Vernice, I'm just their mother. Nearly fifty. Old. Tired.

Lonely. What am I supposed to do? Why should I be told that my son has his bedroom full of guns and God knows what else? Why should I know? Who am I to be talked to? To be told?

VERNICE: Okay, girl. Okay.

MOTHER: It's not okay, it's not! I'm sick of being ignored and pushed around by them; being looked down on. I've got my pride. I've done my fair share of suffering too. I'm sick to death of being criticised by them both. I'm sick! Sick! What the hell do they want?

VERNICE: I don't know.

MOTHER: Well, I'm damned if I do. You know, I just don't care anymore. For the first time in my life I've had it. Up to here. There's just nothing left anyone can do to me anymore. Nothing.

(ALVIN comes downstairs with his flight bag and suitcase.)

VERNICE: Where you going?

ALVIN: I think you've said enough. *(To MOTHER.)* I'm going now.

MOTHER: Going?

ALVIN: Yes, going.

MOTHER: Going where? You've only just come back.

ALVIN: I don't know, mother. I said it was me or you. One of us had to go and I meant it. You didn't tell me, you didn't tell him, I can't live here, I can't live there. What am I supposed to do? What we supposed to do? Live on a raft in the middle of the Atlantic at a point equidistant between Africa, the Caribbean and Britain? Is that what you want us to do? Leave us till we sink? Till there's no trace of us? Lost between two waves, yet another black generation is dispossessed.

MOTHER: What are you talking about? Dispossessed from what?

ALVIN: I've spent the last few hours trying to get some kind of truth into Errol and some kind of truth out of you. I've been stretched tight like a piece of elastic between you both and I haven't a clue which one of you is right. All I know is that I can't be right 'cos I don't know what I'm talking about. Even now as I talk how do I know I'm not talking crap? Things are changing too quickly and all three of us tearing each other to pieces, conflict, conflict, conflict! Everywhere people playing at being something they aren't, everywhere someone so sure, so convinced that they've just got to be wrong. What the hell is going on? You don't know, right? Well, neither do I. The longer I stay here the more strain there's going to be and eventually I'll snap. I'll flip out and end up like Errol.

MOTHER: What do you mean end up like Errol?

ALVIN: Where do you think he's going? Africa? We might as well start digging his grave now.

MOTHER: Alvin!

ALVIN: Listen. He hasn't even got a passport.

MOTHER: But he applied for one. He has a passport.

ALVIN: Mother, mother, mother. When they asked him his nationality he put down… He put down African. And place of birth? The Dark Continent. They must have died laughing in the passport office.

MOTHER: Well, what's he going to do?

ALVIN: Errol's twenty-one and he can swim, after a fashion, for a while at least. Then, unless something happens, he'll sink.

MOTHER: Alvin! He's your brother!

ALVIN: And my dad was your husband! I've said all I've got to say.

MOTHER: Alvin! For Christ's sake, I've done my best. What do you want? What is it you all want from me?

ALVIN: From you, mother, nothing. You've got nothing left to give me. None of you have.

MOTHER: But you're all I've got. You're all I've lived for…

ALVIN: Sorry, mother.

(He turns and goes via the front doorway.)

MOTHER: Alvin! I'll do anything for you all, you know that. Alvin? Alvin!

(She cries.)

VERNICE: It's no use, girl. He's gone. They've both gone.

MOTHER: Oh my God!

VERNICE: They'll be back, don't worry.

MOTHER: No they won't. They won't be back. Oh my God!

VERNICE: They will. Vivien. Stop it. Tears ain't goin' help. I tell you that before. Why you not come over an' sit with me, nuh?

MOTHER: Jesus Lord Almighty, help me! Help me!

VERNICE: Come on now, girl. Come on. Calm down, nuh?

MOTHER: Vernice, leave me alone, please.

VERNICE: I don't think me should, girl.

MOTHER: Please leave me alone. I'll be alright now. Could you just please get me a glass of water and I'll be alright.

(VERNICE goes through and gets it.)

121

VERNICE: Look, girl, if me leave you I going come back in an hour. *(She comes back through.)* I have to make up Charmain's tea and give she some spending money then I goin' come back.

MOTHER: I'll be alright.

VERNICE: Sure?

MOTHER: Sure I'm sure.

VERNICE: Well. Gimme a smile, nuh. *(MOTHER gives her a faint smile.)* It goin' come alright. By tomorrow you done forget the whole thing an' everything goin' back to normal.

MOTHER: Alright.

VERNICE: I see you then, girl. I jus' go see to she.

MOTHER: Alright… Vernice?

VERNICE: What?

MOTHER: Thanks for everything. I don't know how I'd have managed without you.

VERNICE: *(Sucks teeth.)* Girl, you jus' start to learn at last. We got to stick together, nuh?

(She goes. MOTHER remains motionless for a few moments after the back door has shut. She looks across at Wallace's picture on the cabinet. She moves very slowly and with great dignity. She gets up and goes round to the drawer. She takes her glass of water with her. She takes out two bottles of pills, empties some into her hand and swallows them. She takes a drink. She repeats until both bottles are empty. She comes back round and sits on the settee, her body heaving with tears. She leans over the arm of the settee and doesn't move anymore.

a key at the door. MOTHER doesn't respond. ALVIN comes
resumes her asleep. He puts down his bags and goes across
binet where he takes the broken picture of her and looks at
mes across and stands over her. He can't say anything. He
ck and puts the picture in his bag and takes out the bottle of
He comes across and places it beside her. He kisses her on the
the head. He can't see her face. He picks up his bag and goes.

ts down.)

END OF PLAY

By the same author

Rough Crossings
From the novel by Simon Schama
9781840028041

Coming soon

Caryl Phillips: Plays One
Strange Fruit / Where There is Darkness / The Shelter
9781786827906

WWW.OBERONBOOKS.COM

Follow us on Twitter @oberonbooks
& Facebook @OberonBooksLondon